mmorano@depaul.edu

Grammar Lessons

sightline books

The Iowa Series in Literary Nonfiction

Patricia Hampl & Carl H. Klaus, series editors

Michele Morano
Grammar Lessons
Translating a Life in Spain

For Jeanne-Marie —
With many thanks.
Buena suerte,
Michele Morano
7.24.07

University of Iowa Press, Iowa City

University of Iowa Press, Iowa City 52242
Copyright © 2007 by Michele Morano
www.uiowapress.org
All rights reserved
Printed in the United States of America
Text design by Richard Hendel
No part of this book may be reproduced or used
in any form or by any means without permission in
writing from the publisher. All reasonable steps have
been taken to contact copyright holders of material
used in this book. The publisher would be pleased
to make suitable arrangements with any whom it
has not been possible to reach. While all the events
described here are true, some people's names and
identifying characteristics have been changed in the
interest of privacy.

Lines from "Do That to Me One More Time"
copyright © Toni Tennille, used by permission.

The University of Iowa Press is a member of
Green Press Initiative and is committed to
preserving natural resources.
Printed on acid-free paper

LCCN: 2006932733
ISBN-10: 1-58729-530-X
ISBN-13: 978-1-58729-530-0

07 08 09 10 11 C 5 4 3 2 1

What would I be without language? My existence has been determined by language, not only the spoken, but the unspoken, the language of speech and the language of motion.

— SIMON J. ORTIZ

Contents

Preface

The essays in this collection are born of the idea that grammar is spacious, encompassing not just the rules of spoken and written language but all the other modes of communication that help us negotiate the world in which we live. I began to think of grammar this way some years ago while living in Spain, teaching English at the University of Oviedo, and learning to speak Spanish. During that time I wrestled daily with vocabulary lists, verb tense, and rules whose exceptions continually escaped me, and I taught students who had as much trouble with a new language as I did. We communicated using all the available tools — textbooks, dictionaries, pantomime, pictures, even movies, music, and food. In the classroom, grammar began with the words on the page, but it was much, much larger than that.

This was true outside the classroom as well. As my language ability improved, my perspective on grammar broadened, especially once I began to develop close friendships. One way we get to know each other is by telling personal stories, and in order to understand my friends' stories, it wasn't enough to listen closely to their words, to the shape of their sentences. I also had to pay attention to their gestures and mannerisms, to the atmosphere of the cafés in which we spoke, to the rhythm of a night spent wandering through the historic part of town, stopping for wine, for tapas (called *pinchos* in the North), for the regional specialty of hard cider, and returning again and again to sidewalks that bustled at midnight, at 4:00 AM, at daybreak. "The Spanish live on the street," everyone kept telling me, until I could feel the street and the patterns of life it governed in even the smallest forms of communication.

Telling my own stories in Spanish made me keenly aware of the connections between grammatical rules and the conceptual frameworks that help us understand experience. Here's a very small example: In Spanish, one doesn't *drop* an object; either one *throws* the object intentionally, or the object *falls*. Linguistically, the phrase *cayó de mis manos*—fell from my hands—was easy enough to master, but conceptually, because I was used to blaming myself whenever, say, my keys landed on the floor, speaking correctly involved changing the way I thought. This happened over and over again. As I shared stories with friends, negotiating the opportunities and constraints of Spanish, I experienced tiny moments of revision, moments when translating past events into the present meant altering just slightly the way I understood things. Eventually even the backdrop of my life in Spain—the music, the architecture, the frequent, luxurious pauses built into the day—seemed to affect the way I told stories. And, ultimately, the sense I made of them.

Travel, after all, involves a continual process of translation and interpretation, not only of words but of body language, landscapes, works of art, historical sites, the list goes on. Even remembering is an act of translation—between the past and the present, visual images and their verbal counterparts, reality and imagination. No wonder, then, that the roots of the word *grammar* in both Latin and Greek are connected to *art*, to the process of ingesting experience, working it over in the mind, transforming the results into something both larger and truer than the raw material one starts with.

I was reminded of this idea recently, on a return visit to Spain, while touring the small Cantabrian village of Santillana del Mar. In the middle of a summer day, I took refuge from the sun in a gift shop whose thick stone walls kept the air refreshingly cool. A few other tourists milled about, all of us browsing silently as the radio played the sultry 1970s love song, "Do That to Me One More Time." Soon the middle-aged proprietor began to sing along, and then an older German gentleman joined in. They didn't understand most of the English words, so they hummed and imitated the vowel sounds, their deep voices harmonizing with Toni Tennille in a way that stirred them both. I turned toward a display case to hide my smile, wondering where each man had been when the song came out, to what fields of memory he was transported by the song's refrain: "Do that to me one more time/ Once is never enough/ with a man like you/ Oh-oh, do that to me one more time/ I can never get enough/ from a man like you." Their voices lingered over each "you," drawing it out to two syllables, and as I struggled not to laugh I suddenly found myself blinking back tears.

The song summons in me all the cloying emotions of adolescence, the age when I first heard it. Even so, erase the literal meaning, pay attention only to the richness of the voice, the slow, sweet rhythm and minor chords, and it's a stunning piece of music. Add the spontaneous sounds of two men who don't share a common language, who might not sing as energetically if they understood the lyrics, and the scene becomes an emblem of how little our words sometimes matter as we move about in the world, connecting with one another. The two men conversed about beauty and pleasure and the insistent way the past makes itself felt in the present, and I understood them perfectly. The other tourists in the shop seemed to understand as well. Beside me an elderly woman smiled, her fingers tapping lightly against a display case. Near the door, her husband stood gazing out into a cobblestone plaza, his body swaying. We all listened, connected by subtle vibrations, by the grammar of the moment. There are lessons in this scene, I thought, looking forward to a time in the future when I might make sense of them.

Travel, for me, is always about lessons, about learning what can't be taught in a classroom. Travel is about observing, interacting, ingesting; it's about making oneself vulnerable in new contexts and then, afterwards, through a combination of memory and imagination, coming to a place of insight. Often it takes months or years before I begin to comprehend what I've learned from a journey, and, as the essays in this collection illustrate, language and storytelling play key roles in that process. At the same time, these essays—all of which deal in some fashion with my relationship to Spain—are concerned less with arrivals than with departures, passages, and reflections. Their focus is on the glimpses of meaning that travel experiences can offer and that true stories, artfully told, can help us understand.

The essays of *Part One, Oviedo,* stem from the pivotal time I spent living in Spain, during which I struggled—often humorously—to learn the language, absorb the culture, and balance a temporary, thrilling existence against the emotional weight of the life I'd left behind in the United States. The essays of *Part Two, Madrid, Altamira, Guernica,* revolve around later trips to Spain and explore questions raised by my personal travel history and by the historical and artistic legacies of place. The essays of *Part Three*, *After Spain*, reflect on travel in the broadest sense, from literal movement along highways to metaphoric movement through stages of understanding, and they illuminate some of the quirky and poignant language lessons that can shape sensibility. All together, the stories in this collection describe one woman's journey through many kinds of grammar toward a deeper sense of her place in the world. In the process, I hope they do justice to the importance—and the difficulty—of identifying, adjusting to, and sometimes changing the conceptual borders within which we live.

Part One. Oviedo

Ca Beleño

he language course was for *extranjeros*: foreigners or, as I preferred to translate the word, strangers. Many of us had come alone to northern Spain, and we congregated every day at 4:00 PM, eager to get our bearings and learn how to talk about them. In the humid September classroom we compared notes on the beguiling streets of Oviedo, on the historic district with its medieval buildings and plazas and markets — the fish market, the market filled with fresh vegetables from the nearby countryside. It was easy to get lost in that section of town, and we all did, every day. But sometimes we made discoveries, too, and word of a great café called Bar Sevilla, or a tiny store that sold only umbrellas, spread during the breaks in our lessons.

During class, we extranjeros observed each other carefully, noting the differences in our clothing and mannerisms and generalizing about the cultures from which we'd come. The Germans were the outdoor folks, organizing hikes and biking trips each weekend, while the Dutch assimilated effortlessly, making Spanish friends, it seemed, every time they left the house. The French students admitted to the most nationalistic pride, one day bringing in a stack of warm crepes wrapped in tinfoil, which they distributed with tiny packets of sugar. A group of outgoing Italians entertained everyone with their sing-song accents, while we Americans — a graduate student named Michael and I — were so intent on learning Spanish that we refused to speak English with each other, even when the alternative was comic pantomime.

There were also lone representatives from Japan, Turkey, Russia, Australia, and above all, Denmark. At some point I must have been introduced to the Danish Guy, a shy, handsome man with broad shoulders and wire-rimmed glasses, but I don't remember his name.

I only remember his face, his mannerisms, the quiet movements of his body. And the way I kept an eye on him every afternoon, admiring his facial expressions, the sound of his voice. The attraction was a pleasant, daily surprise, something familiar in the foreignness of acclimating to a new place. Seeing the Danish Guy each afternoon, feeling my face flush when he looked my way, was as thrilling as walking down the street and glimpsing my own reflection in a plate glass window, rippled over by Spanish words.

In those early weeks, before the regular academic year began, before I started to teach in the evenings and tutor privately in the mornings, the language course gave shape and purpose to the days. Almost from the moment I arrived in Oviedo, I had a life, a legitimate existence there, and I transferred my gratitude for that to the other extranjeros. Especially the French students. I loved running into them outside class, hearing my name called at an intersection and turning to see Henri waving his long arms over his head, or standing in line at the grocery store and feeling the tickle of Sophie's fingers on the back of my neck. The French students and I felt the kind of bonding that comes with intense new situations — summer camp or the first weeks of a difficult job — but we also really liked each other, approved of each other in a way that felt born of good fortune.

One Sunday in late September, I'd met up with the French students for an afternoon drink at Bar Sevilla. It was raining that day, and we'd dripped all over each other as we settled around a tiny table, communicating with our limited vocabulary and lots of hand motions. Henri, Jules, and Christophe were quick to laugh and flirt — with me, with each other, with the waiter who brought our glasses of beer, and with their compatriots, Danielle and Sophie. Danielle flirted back, while Sophie asked questions about me, about my teaching appointment, my life in the United States, the boyfriend I'd left behind. Sophie wore round, tortoise-shell glasses and had a habit of drawing her lips together in a pout whether she agreed or disagreed or was simply pondering. When her friends lapsed back into French, she pouted intensely and, gesturing toward me, gave them a stern, "Español, por favor."

As the afternoon slid toward evening, the aromas of a Spanish bar — smoked ham, sardines, tobacco, espresso — began to work on my sense of the future. I listened to the rain pattering on the sidewalk, sampled from tiny plates of olives, and felt ecstatic with possibility, with all the experiences I might stumble into in the months ahead. The French students emboldened me with their poise, their lack of self-consciousness as travelers. They pulled me into their ironic banter, even in the unformed way we all spoke, without bothering to conjugate verbs. What we had to say to each other then was so broad, so introductory that grammar seemed almost beside the point, and getting to know one another without full access to language seemed entirely possible.

Later, when we waved good-bye across the cathedral plaza, squinting through rain that fell like confetti, I felt flushed, excited, a little bit in love.

During that initial period in Oviedo, each day felt like falling in love. I was breathless, giddy, fragile, aware. Everything attracted me: the patterned sidewalks, a tiny kiosk selling magazines and bus tickets, peacocks preening for each other in the park. Morning and evening, I wandered through the city, trying to memorize its angles and curves, its cathedral bells weighted with the cadence of nostalgia.

And I really was in love, not only in the metaphorical sense that travel often brings but literally, with the man I'd left behind in New York. Each morning I walked downtown to the university's Office of International Relations where we extranjeros collected our mail and where, once or twice a week, a letter waited for me. With my heartbeat thumping against my eardrums, I'd grasp the letter and descend three flights of marble stairs, then step onto the sidewalk and check the sky. On rainy days I'd duck into a nearby café, and on clear days, or during breaks in the showers that came more frequently throughout the fall, I'd hurry to the cathedral plaza and sit on a bench, on a folded newspaper if the seat was still wet.

In that time just before the Internet transformed long-distance communication, I read letters as I wrote them — slowly, paying attention to every word. I savored his optimism or, more often, absorbed his dismay, taking deep breaths and reminding myself that there wasn't much I could do for him from here. Sometimes I wrote back immediately, describing the landscape, how city buildings suddenly part, exposing a view of jagged peaks to the south. How from just behind the train station, Naranco Mountain rises lush and green, and how from its summit Oviedo shimmers below like Oz. Sometimes I related funny or embarrassing mistakes I'd made with the language, and sometimes I just thought about what to say in response, about how to negotiate the truth of missing him terribly and, at the same time, feeling unforgivably happy to be alone. Sitting on my bench or in the window of a café, I imagined response after potential response, minutes ticking away until the cathedral bells filled the plaza like a hymn.

One Friday morning in October, when the sky was unusually clear and the breeze warm and soft, I ran into Sophie as I crossed the plaza toward my favorite bench. "We never talk anymore," she moaned, clasping my hands in hers. She was taking political science courses in the mornings by then, and I was teaching English in the evenings, and although we saw each other every afternoon in the class for extranjeros, we rarely had time to chat. I missed Sophie, and I agreed that we should get together soon.

"Why not tonight?" she asked, shaking my fingers in hers. "Why not come to Ca Beleño for a drink with me? You've never been there, you know, not once."

It was true. I hadn't been to Ca Beleño, the bar where the extranjeros gathered, and this wasn't the first time someone had called me on it. Bars in Spain are brightly lit places where juice, soda, coffee, or tea is as common an order as alcohol. But the stories I'd heard about Ca Beleño made it sound more like an American frat bar, where people drank to get drunk and took easy offense. I'd avoided Ca Beleño for the same reasons I avoided the McDonald's on Calle Uría—even when I had a craving for American-style fries—because it seemed inauthentic, like cheating. Sophie listened as I detailed the rumor of a recent fistfight, and responded with her usual pout. "Yes, well, that did happen, it's true. But it was caused by some English soccer fans on their way to Barcelona. Look, we'll have one drink and go elsewhere before anyone gets drunk, I promise." Then she leaned in until our foreheads nearly touched. "Meet me there at 11:00 tonight. Please? Because there's something I need to talk to you about." Her stance and the tone of her voice were so intimate I agreed. Only later did it occur to me that the Danish Guy might show up at Ca Beleño too.

On a Friday night in Spain, 11:00 PM is still dinnertime. In another hour, people would begin the transition, meeting up with friends for coffee, then moving on to a series of bars and then, at 3:00 or 4:00 in the morning, to a dance floor. So I was surprised to see groups of patrons, some of them clearly Spanish, in the Ca Beleño courtyard. They sat on benches and leaned against the wrought-iron fence, drinks and cigarettes in their hands. From the shadows one of the German students called my name, and when I stepped forward he exclaimed, "You're finally here!" I waved awkwardly, unsure how to respond to a comment that both welcomed and chastised.

The front door of Ca Beleño looked down a set of stairs into a bright cloud of smoke. Around the room's perimeter were tables and booths, and in every meter of floor space between, people crowded together. At the rear, Sophie stood on the rung of a barstool, thrusting her arm above her head to get my attention. I plunged into the crowd, into a dizzying array of familiar faces, including a number of Spanish people I knew — students, university workers, friends of friends — and the Danish Guy, who smiled broadly as he said hello. Flustered, I kept going, with so many people calling me by name and kissing my cheeks that I began to feel like Young Goodman Brown discovering the secret meeting place of the community. Ca Beleño was the dark forest of Oviedo and resisting my place in it suddenly seemed futile.

When I reached Sophie, she was ordering four *carajillos*, goblets of coffee and bourbon topped with fresh whipped cream and slender cookies. I helped her carry them to a table occupied by Christophe and one of the Italians. "It's about time you joined us here," Christophe scolded as I sat down, and the Italian agreed, adding something in such fast and fluid Spanish I didn't understand. Before I could respond, Sophie gestured for him to move over so she could sit near me. "We need to talk," she announced conspiratorially.

Later I would understand that on this night Sophie was already in love with the Italian, and that she had already glimpsed the pain, if not the outright danger, their entanglement would cause her. Later I'd see that she wanted to talk to me, of all people, because she was concerned about a relationship that might one day span two countries. That's what we do when we're in love — we look for models, for evidence in the people around us that the storyline we're following can have a happy ending. We anchor our hopes for the future on signs and premonitions and anything else that might bridge the gap between desire and uncertainty. But I didn't realize this then, and so I was baffled by Sophie's sudden interest in my situation.

She began by saying she didn't want to pry, and I could tell her if she was, but back on that first afternoon in Bar Sevilla, didn't I say something about a man in New York, a boyfriend? I said yes, I'd mentioned him then, and yes, we were still together. Sophie smiled and nodded. "Then there are some things I want to ask you. Some things I want to understand, OK?" A few tables away, just over Sophie's shoulder in my line of vision, sat the Danish Guy. He, too, was sipping a carajillo, accompanied by the Dutch women, their Spanish boyfriends, and two German men. They all seemed to be having a good time, the Danish Guy laughing now and then with his usual restraint.

Sophie leaned in close and, raising her voice over the music, asked whether it was hard being away from the man in New York. I said it was. She asked if he planned to visit me, and I said yes, just after Christmas. I didn't tell her that although he often mentioned the trip in his letters, he hadn't set the dates yet or looked into reservations, and part of me wasn't sure he would really come. Explaining all that required complicated verbs—futures and conditionals and subjunctives—and the likelihood of confusion increased with each one. It's the great paradox of learning a new language that as we become more adept at speaking, we also become more daunted by the complexity of what we want to say.

Sophie turned to the past. She asked how we met, what he studied, how long we'd been dating, and I answered these questions with ease. We'd been together for two years. He studied English literature in the same Master's program I graduated from. He wasn't sure yet what he'd do afterward, just as I didn't know what I'd do when I moved back to the States in the summer.

"What about you?" I asked. "Is there any romance in your life?"

Sophie dismissed my question with a shrug and stubbed out her cigarette. She wanted to know why I'd come to Spain. She couldn't imagine being in love with a man and leaving him to live so far away, even for a year. Did I *really* love him? Then why had I left him?

The expression on her face was even more somber than usual, and I was quiet for a moment, surprised at the grave turn of the conversation. Because I liked Sophie a great deal, and because I hadn't talked with anyone about this for a long time, I wanted to tell her that the relationship was difficult. I wanted to strip away the tactful phrasings, the abstractions, and offer details of his depression, his refusal to seek treatment, my constant, tiresome attempts to cheer him up. I wanted to tell her that I'd left him because I desperately needed to live, for a little while, in a place where I was responsible only for myself.

But I couldn't say any of this because I got stuck on the first verb. The relationship *was* difficult. I wanted the past tense, certainly, since the relationship required so little of me right then. But there are two past tenses in Spanish, and I didn't know which to use. With the preterite, *fue*, the relationship was difficult for a set amount of time, and then it wasn't anymore. With the imperfect, *era*, the situation endured for much longer, with other events punctuating it. During my second month of living in Spain, I understood the grammatical rule. But I didn't know how to apply it to my life.

The cream on my carajillo melted slowly, sinking in caramel rays through the coffee. I watched it, realizing that with Sophie it didn't really matter which past tense I used. Like all the extranjeros, she and I could manage imprecise language—if a phrase came within arm's length, we could usually grasp it. But sometimes language is less about what we can make other people understand than about what we're able to explain to ourselves.

"I came here for this," I finally said, gesturing around us. "To be an extranjera. To be alone and not to be alone, all at once."

Sophie nodded, her face tightened in thought. Behind her, the Danish Guy stood, pushed in his chair, and headed for the door. Sophie lit another cigarette and pouted through the sudden cloud of smoke.

Sophie, I thought, was a keeper. There was a connection between us, an affinity I could imagine blossoming into long-term friendship. I liked all the French students, enjoyed running into them unexpectedly at the cinema, where Jules and Danielle would be smoking in the lobby while Henri saved their seats, or in a club late at night, where Danielle and Christophe would be dancing like pros, her dress floating around her curves, his sport coat opening and closing to the beat, and at a table nearby would be Sophie, pouting as she spoke, making Henri and Jules throw their heads back with laughter. Whenever I saw them as a group, they all looked so chic and together that I longed to be one of them. But it was Sophie I admired most. I liked her style, her mix of casual dress and bright red lipstick, her sardonic humor. It was always a thrill to chat with her for a few minutes on the street or in the cafeteria of the language building. She seemed to feel the same about me, and when a new French student arrived in November, Sophie couldn't wait to introduce us.

Because foreign universities had various arrangements with Oviedo's international program, extranjeros arrived and would eventually leave at odd times. So I didn't pay much attention to the chic new stranger who appeared in the advanced conversation class one day, except to note that the Spanish with which she introduced herself to the instructor seemed perfect. Later, as I crossed the courtyard en route to my evening class, Sophie waved me over. She introduced me as an English teacher from America and Monique as a friend from home. Monique was petite and pretty, with short, stylish hair and a slightly bored expression. She grinned as her eyes flitted down to my shoes and back, then turned fully toward Sophie and began to speak in French. I understood "J'ai faim," but only because she was rubbing her stomach hungrily as she spoke.

Over the next few days, Monique's bored expression turned into an outright mope. Sophie took me aside to explain that Monique had left a boyfriend back home, and it was clear Sophie expected me to feel sympathetic. Instead, I felt angry. I thought, it's only France for God's sake, there are *roads* from here to there. She could at least say hello. And yet, because repulsion can sometimes be a form of attraction, I began to keep an eye on Monique. I looked for her each afternoon, noting her moods and who she talked to before and after class. I watched as she absentmindedly pushed her shoulders back and moved her head in circles, stretching her neck. It was a stunning neck, thin and very white, garnished with a single brushstroke of hair. Her profile was also stunning, with the imperfect beauty of some movie stars: a weak chin highlighted her full lips and high cheekbones. In the hallway at break, Monique smoked with one elbow against her hip, holding the cigarette out as she exhaled delicately toward the ceiling. When she saw me watching and smiled, my face instantly flamed.

At the beginning of the following week, Monique suddenly perked up. I discovered the reason for her mood change by accident one evening, while walking across town from my office to the College of Sciences where I taught. My route wound through the historic district, past the architecture I'd sought out during my first weeks in Oviedo. Now that I'd gotten my bearings in the city, I didn't always hear the cathedral bells, and I'd stopped marveling at the medieval buildings I passed. They had become part of the fabric of my day, landmarks for turning left or right, for gauging whether I had time to stop for coffee before class. But what I did notice as I hurried along on this evening, as the setting sun threw whole streets into shadow, was the light the various structures gave off. The pale yellow stone, the orange roof tiles, and the bright gray of the clouds bathed the whole area in a surreal glow. As I nodded hello to strangers, squeezing past them on skinny sidewalks, there was a crispness to everything I saw, an electricity I could feel in each place where my shoes met the pebbled concrete. I passed through the narrow Bishop's Corridor, turned the corner onto La Rua, and resisted the urge to break out running. Living here, going about my daily business, sometimes filled me to bursting.

Then I glanced across the street toward Bar Sevilla, saw them, and ducked into a candy store as if I'd been heading there all along. At first I thought it was a mistake, because I hadn't once seen Monique talk with the Danish Guy, and because the couple sitting on tall stools at a tall table seemed very much like a couple. I circled the store, feigning interest in some chocolate-covered fruit, then returned to the front window, where I could survey licorice squares and Bar Sevilla with the same angle of my head.

Monique faced the street, her elbows leaning on the table in front of a very large glass of beer. The Danish Guy's seat was angled to the side, his profile more animated than ever before. Monique lowered her eyes and giggled at something he said. He lifted the glass of beer, sipped slowly, and handed it to her. I saw then that his foot rested on the rung of her stool, that the outside of her knee leaned against the inside of his. Around me the reds and greens and oranges of a hundred kinds of candy glowed in the fading daylight. Across the street Monique and the Danish Guy caressed each other's wrists.

Outside, the rain began again, tapping with increasing urgency on my umbrella. As I hurried toward class, I turned the scene over in my mind. How quickly they had paired up! And how quickly Monique had gotten over her sadness. I thought of the single beer, the expressions of surprised pleasure, the bodies fully receptive to each other there in a café window. Their arms and shoulders, their gestures had none of the reserve of a full-blown relationship, none of the very slight clues that there are wounded places in need of protection. I recognized that early stage of infinite possibility, and I felt envious, resentful, but also strangely excited — because the beginnings of love affairs are always exciting, even when they're not our own.

At the busy corner of Calle Marqués de Santa Cruz, I waited for a walk sign, wondering whether the man in New York would follow through on his plan to meet me in Madrid just after Christmas. And if he did, I wondered how I'd appear to observers when with him, how my body would look across the table from his in Toledo, Córdoba, Granada. Or in any of the cafés in this very city, including Bar Sevilla. Would we experience a new beginning, feel the way Monique and the Danish Guy seemed to — excited, enthralled, as if everything we knew about each other was, and would remain, fantastic?

The light turned and a crowd of pedestrians crossed the street, each of us leaping over the flooded gutter onto the curb. Rain danced on the sidewalk ahead, while behind us the cathedral bells began to chime. I listened closely, anticipating each note in the soundtrack of my life here. The bells stirred up an ache I couldn't identify, a haunting, future-tense sorrow: the longing for a time that isn't over yet.

As the calendar year drew toward a close, my attendance in the language class for extranjeros became sporadic. I seemed to learn as much from talking with Spanish friends as from anything else, and some days I preferred lingering over the midday meal to rushing off to class. As a result, by December I was seeing much less of the other extranjeros — except for Monique and the Danish Guy, who seemed to be everywhere. In the late afternoon they leaned against a bar drinking coffee, his broad shoulders angled protectively toward her small body. Or they relaxed on a bench in San Francisco Park, her hand resting on his thigh. Or they appeared at the cinema, in the stationery section of a department store, on the corner of Calle Uría as I rode past on a bus. And one morning, on my way to the open-air market, I saw them outside a bookstore gesturing fiercely toward each other, keeping their voices low but with tempers clearly flaring. Instinctively I crossed to the other side of the street and monitored their reflection in a shop window.

That argument troubled me for days, and I discovered I'd been narrating their relationship to myself since I first spied on them from the candy store. Without realizing it, I'd been making interpretations: that their attraction to each other was instantaneous, that they'd been secretive about it until Monique settled the matter back in France, that their initial, intense feelings had given way to a comfortable intimacy. They were a romantic pair, but also a practical, level-headed one. They were perfect, really, with no deep sadness between them, no mood swings to counter, no ominous silences to decode.

And now this. Of course I'd expected disagreements, but not there on the sidewalk, not with such a display of anger. This wasn't part of the script I'd written for them. I felt haunted by what I'd seen and dismayed to think that Monique and the Danish Guy might have broken up.

My own situation had become more promising by then. He'd booked a flight to Madrid and reserved a rental car for our two-week vacation. His letters seemed hopeful about the holidays, about our trip, about the future. I began to think, at first tentatively and then with more conviction, that reward rather than punishment would follow this period of solitary bliss. And then, as if in confirmation of my optimism, I ran into Monique and the Danish Guy in the hall outside the English department, smiling and holding hands.

One Friday afternoon in mid December, Sophie phoned me with a strange tone to her voice. "Don't worry, it's nothing too bad," she said, sensing my alarm. "It's just that I haven't seen you for a while, and I wanted to make sure you came to Ca Beleño tonight to say good-bye to *los franceses*." Back in the beginning, when December seemed an impossible time away, I'd known that the French students would return to France before Christmas, but I couldn't believe we'd reached that time already. Sophie said everyone was leaving tomorrow, that she alone would come back in January. "You and me, we're here until the end," she said, a note of relief in her voice.

We arrived at Ca Beleño before 9:30 PM. The place was nearly empty, so we were able to push several tables together and sit comfortably around them. All evening extranjeros would be stopping in to say good-bye to the French students, buying them drinks and wishing them well, but at the beginning our group was only a little bigger than it had been that first Sunday in Bar Sevilla. There were the people who were leaving: Danielle, Jules, Henri, and Christophe. And then there were the people I resolved to see more in the new year, before it was time for all of us to go: Michael and his Spanish girlfriend, Sophie and her Italian boyfriend.

Before long, Sophie's boyfriend and I got into an argument about the quality of fresh fruits and vegetables in Spain. While he lambasted the country's produce, I hotly defended the open-air market and Spanish cuisine in general. Everyone laughed at the rigor of our debate, and we laughed harder still when Michael's girlfriend began to correct the Italian's vocabulary. Finally I could see why I had trouble understanding him: half the words he used when speaking Spanish were actually Italian. I asked Sophie if this were true, and she rolled her eyes. "If only I spoke Italian," she said, "we would communicate much better in Spanish." Her boyfriend threw his head back with laughter, then kissed her cheek. But when he went to the bar for more drinks, Sophie leaned toward me, an anguished look on her face. "You and I will talk one day," she said, motioning toward him with her chin. "This is very difficult. You understand? *He* is very difficult."

Soon Ca Beleño filled with smoke and with voices that shouted above the music. Our group grew and shifted, losing a table and some chairs in the process, the toasts coming one after another. "To Oviedo!" someone said, and we drank. "To the mountains!" "To King Juan Carlos!" "To Ca Beleño!" At the far end of the table, Danielle had one arm around Michael and the other around his girlfriend, and all three were singing in a language I couldn't identify.

People came and went, moving between the excessive heat inside and the crisp air of the courtyard. Sophie and I shared a seat, our elbows linked for balance. Jules stood surveying the crowd, and when our eyes met he smiled broadly and raised his glass. "To Me-shell," he said. "When I think of you I'll always remember the day of the marvelous rain." Christophe called out, "Rain? Was there a day without it?" and everyone laughed. Henri winked and Sophie squeezed my shoulder and Jules continued to smile. Then many glasses rose into the air, a salute, and we all drank to an afternoon in common, to the rain and Bar Sevilla and that early stage of infinite possibility.

When Monique arrived, there was a chorus of "hola" and "por fin"—finally! She was smiling, but there was a studied indifference in her eyebrows, in the set of her jaw, that made my stomach tighten. Monique had been in Oviedo for only six weeks, and I assumed that meant she was staying until spring. But now I saw that I'd been wrong, that she was leaving too.

The Danish Guy arrived shortly after, wearing the same insistently jocular expression. He squeezed Monique's shoulders and leaned over to say hello, then moved about, chatting with Henri, putting his arm around Jules, who handed him a glass of beer and offered a toast. Eventually, after circling the whole group, the Danish Guy perched on the edge of Monique's chair. They shared the space in a way that looked polite, and I could see that they were already drawing apart, already deferring to the rest of each other's lives.

Henri wanted everyone to finish their drinks and head to Santa Sebe for dancing. "It's our last night, why should we sleep?" he asked repeatedly. I watched as the Danish Guy asked Monique a question, watched as she shook her head. He stood up and motioned toward the door, and she shook her head again. Then there was an awful pause, and everything in the bar seemed to stop, go quiet. She had one hand on the edge of the table, the other arm flung over the back of the chair. His face was the slightest bit imploring but moving toward resolve. Then he bent over and kissed the top of her head, and made his way toward the door without looking back.

I turned to Sophie, who was watching me as intently as I'd been watching Monique. To Sophie, whose own romantic relationship would, in a few months' time, quite literally almost kill her. We stared at each other and shook our heads, filled our cheeks with air and held it for a moment, then exhaled slowly. Across the table Monique lit a cigarette. She took a drag and blew, took a drag and blew. Then, abruptly, she stubbed out the cigarette and headed for the door, and I wondered: is it ever possible to fall in love and not pay for it later on?

One by one people stood up, swallowing the last of their drinks. Sophie said she'd call me as soon as she was back in town and hopefully get to meet the man from New York. Jules clapped me on the back and asked, "To Santa Sebe?" I smiled and said no. "But it will be the last time you'll see us in that bar," he pleaded, and Christophe chimed in, "The last time you'll see us anywhere!" Danielle approached with a pen and notebook and asked for my address. She said she wasn't a very good correspondent but she'd like to send a card sometime, and I said the same was true for me. Then came the good-byes, with so many people kissing both cheeks of so many other people—and Christophe and Henri kissing each other over and over—that I was able to get away without too much cajoling.

Outside in the crisp December air, a couple held one another on a bench in the shadows, their heads closely bowed. I expected it to be Monique and the Danish Guy, and I wanted it to be because that seemed like a good ending, for their story and for mine. Instead, it was Michael and his Spanish girlfriend, a couple who would stay together through the academic year and then, in June, move together to Boston to the surprise of everyone who knew them.

The street that led toward my neighborhood was dark and empty, and I hurried along, my mind filled with the French students. Danielle and Christophe and Henri and Jules, four people whose presence I'd enjoyed every time I'd been with them. They *amused* me, I thought in Spanish, in that imperfect past tense, and I understood that Jules was right: I wouldn't run into them at Santa Sebe ever again. I wouldn't stop to chat with them in the hall outside my office or in the plaza in front of the cathedral, our voices competing with the bells. And that seemed a terrible shame. It wasn't that I wished I'd become better friends with them or that I regretted not accepting more of their invitations. It wasn't that I wanted anything more with them than what I'd had. But already I missed what I'd had.

There is more than one way to say "I miss" in Spanish, but the most common way in Spain is an idiomatic expression that's impossible to translate. *Echo de menos* combines the verb "to throw" with the adjective for "less." The phrase makes no literal sense, but emotionally it captures the convoluted feelings of displacement that can occur even when it's not you who goes away. I would have missed the French students in English, too, or in any other language we happened to have lived in. But this particular missing was Spanish, tied to Asturias, to Oviedo, to a time when we'd come together there as strangers and enhanced one another's sense of the future.

The intersection up ahead shone under a streetlamp. I hurried toward it, then stood waiting for a single car to pass while my imagination continued on—down the block and around the corner, up the elevator to the fifth floor apartment. I imagined closing the door of my bedroom and sobbing into a pillow, adjusting to the kind of loss that travel always brings. There's no way around this, I told myself. If you move about in the world, if you live fully and fall in love—with friends and acquaintances and places and periods of time—your heart is going to break again and again. Each time you say good-bye, you'll feel the ache of impermanence, of inevitability, of your own terribly finite days.

I turned away from the approaching car, clenching my jaw and thinking again, "What a shame." To the left was a bread shop I frequented by day, and in the streetlamp's glow I noticed the red cursive letters painted on its glass door. *Panadería* they declared, like a password or a magic phrase. I stared at the word, puzzling over its effect until a guilty thrill spread up from the base of my spine and fluttered against my throat. "I'm in Spain," I said aloud to the empty street. "I am still in Spain." And then by way of proof, I saw beyond the strange beauty of the letters to my own amazed reflection watching back from the shadows.

The Queimada

And later, after the mussels, after the *pulpo a la gallega*, the swirling bits of octopus flesh in a sauce of garlic and tomatoes, after the glasses of wine and loaves of bread broken and passed hand to hand, after the strong local blue cheese spread thick on thin crackers and the apples drizzled with honey, after we have all eaten as much as we can and then picked the remains from one another's plates, tucking into our mouths one more bite, one more spoonful, one more tangy or sweet or salty fingertip, then we turn, lights dimmed and candles aflame, to the Queimada.

In the kitchen Chus shows me the brown ceramic bottle, the label handwritten: Aguardiente. I say it aloud. The other words I cannot pronounce because they are in the dialect of Galicia, the province where Chus was born. He is the only Gallego among us, the only person with roots in the land of magic and spirits, of incantations. Chus opens the bottle, holds it out for me to smell, explains that this is liquor made from the skins of grapes, not quite wine, not quite whiskey, and stronger than either. May I taste it, I ask, and Chus smiles, not yet, not until we tame it with fire.

His smile is full, expectant. In this apartment, which is not where he lives but where he spends his extra time with a dozen other artists, painting, sculpting, developing photographs, Chus is more himself than anywhere else. I have seen him in bars, at the homes of mutual friends, on the street as he heads off to work, and nowhere else does he look quite so full, quite so content. And above all tonight, a night on which he has brought this group together—his coworkers from the newspaper, their partners and friends—to share food and drink and the experience of calling spirits to us.

Around the table there is silence and arms resting on stomachs. Moonlight outlines the window shades, outlines Chus positioning the large clay bowl in the middle of the table. I say that the moon is full on the winter solstice, imagine, and the others sigh yes, how amazing. I arrived with a full moon, I do not say, and I will see six more, perhaps seven, and then I will leave. I am already nostalgic, already sad for the day I arrived here, so impressionable and with so much faith. And sad for this night, too, which I am already imagining as memory, the night of my first Queimada in a cold apartment on Calle Independencia, Oviedo, Spain.

And then we begin. Chus says to me, the foreigner, the person for whom every ritual is new: Pretend we're on a beach. The waves are rolling into the shore, the sand is moving under our feet. We can feel the spirits rushing in the wind, listening to our pleas. His eyes move around the table, to Lola, to Begoña and Pascual, to Isabel and her eight-year-old daughter Virginia, to Alberto, to Pilar, to me. He waits until we are all focused intently on him. And then he smiles and shrugs and begins.

The wooden ladle brims at the level of our eyes. Pilar lights a match, and we inhale as the fire erupts, pulsing over the ladle, dripping down and across the surface of the sugared Aguardiente in the bowl. Chus stirs carefully before scooping again, lifting and holding and releasing a long blue stream of liquid fire. Over and over, the motion in his wrist hypnotic, he stirs and lifts and spills, finding a rhythm that the words begin to ride.

Three months ago, I did not understand the language here. I listened to the words and sometimes understood them but not the language, not at all. Spanish. Castellano. And then early one morning in a lighted bar when I was tired from a long day, a day of taking Spanish classes and teaching English classes and making my way through the unfamiliar streets, Lola and Pilar talked and I listened to the sounds like short, lapping waves. The table was round, I remember, and small. They smoked Ducados, lighting and exhaling, waving their hands, and I drifted off as in a dream. In this dream I could hear their words, and the words came not singly but in pairs or triangles and then in long lines that slipped by inseparable. The lines floated around me, background noises circling closer and closer, until words draped themselves in sentences upon and around and within my mind and there, in a brightly lit bar at 5:00 AM with Lola and Pilar laughing, the dialogue sprang alive and I understood.

Now I listen and the words float through me in phrases that will never make sense. Now I look around at the faces, the slight smiles, closed eyes, the full-stomached belief in the power of rituals even though not one of us understands what is happening here. Even Chus does not understand, or remember, all of what he's trying to say. This is a poem, a prayer to the dark spirits, a rhyme he tries to call back from the depths of memory. In place of certain lines, he hums, the rhythm held deep within his throat, within the motion of his arm and shoulder. Our faces are beginning to glisten, and I am memorizing the movements, listening to the almost familiar sounds, like Castellano but not quite, like the language of my sleeping dreams, always on the verge of being remembered. The sounds swirl and lift and pour and burn, and I am so open, so thankful for the warmth and the transport back into the part of my mind where language rises and falls like fire dancing on liquid, that I don't notice Chus is humming and humming, dissolving with the last line, the final word, into laughter.

And later, after the fire has calmed itself, after our faces have turned red and we have dabbed them with napkins, after we have pushed back our chairs and Isabel's eight-year-old daughter Virginia has come to stand beside me, beside the only other person as amazed as she is, Chus covers the bowl with a white cloth and in a moment there is only the liquid, warm and sweet. And familiar. I drink from a ceramic cup with no handle and nod to Chus. Yes, I like it. Yes, it's strong. I rub my stomach where the heat pools. Alberto puts his hand on my shoulder, jostling me in the rough way he jostles everyone. You'll be a Spaniard soon, his mustache smiles, and everyone smiles, at me, at each other, at the middle of the table. And yes, it seems possible that I may become a Spaniard. That I may be transformed entirely by this place and these people whose goal one Friday night each month is to gather together, to eat and drink and introduce the American room-mate of Lola to some specialty of this land. Last month it was cheese, ten kinds of cheese from the region of Asturias, and *sidra*, hard cider poured from a bottle held over the head into a glass held below the hip. Everyone marveled at how much I love sidra, and I couldn't tell them that it wasn't the taste at all, that the taste was neither here nor there, something one gets accustomed to, but rather it was the feeling. Drinking sidra, every time, my body turns into a sponge. Even before the alcohol can take hold, my shoulders broaden, my hips relax, I expand.

Or the month before, paella. Gazpacho. Red wines from Andalucía. Hard green olives stuffed with anchovies, fried sardines. And in months to come, Spanish tortillas, Spanish crepes, sangría. Deep-fried onions which Lola and I will spend an entire day stuffing with tuna fish. We will skip the month of January because Chus and Begoña and Pascual will be skiing in France, but as the spring moves on we will rearrange our schedules, plan and cajole and set aside the time because the time will be moving more quickly, and this will be our way of marking it. Our way of making sure it doesn't get ahead of us, of measuring the months by the stacks of dishes in the sink, by the number of people we squeeze around the dining room table.

As the liquid cools, it thickens. I sip and kiss, drawing my lips together and slowly apart. Syrup builds on the rim of my cup, on all the cups and on all the mouths glistening in the candlelight. Begoña rests an arm on Pascual's knees, Lola strokes Virginia's hair, Chus leans back, legs extended beneath the table, hands clasped across his chest. We are full.

My thoughts rise and fall, bobbing through months and moments, coming to rest finally at the darkening end of a cold day last week. I was walking along the northern edge of the Campo de San Francisco where the kiosks selling Christmas wares made me homesick for something I couldn't identify, something I've never even had. The bag on my shoulder was heavy, my coat was heavy as well, though not particularly warm, and I felt small within my skin, aware that with each step I took things rattled loose inside me.

And then, miraculously, a new kiosk appeared up ahead, at the corner of the park. An older woman dressed in a blue coat gestured toward the setting sun, toward the mountains where she'd collected the chestnuts, and I nodded as she rolled a piece of newspaper into a cone, filled it, and took the 150 pesetas I handed her. Chestnuts! I nearly burst out laughing, walking slowly and then more quickly, with no destination in mind. One by one I extracted them, pulled away the hulls, held the warm flesh on my tongue. I walked for a long time, delighting in the texture and the taste, in the practicality of the newspaper and my good fortune.

Now, as I settle into the fullness, I think it is for this that I travel, for this that I sold all my belongings and took off for a place I didn't know. These moments, walking through a park eating chestnuts, sitting at this table where by now no one is speaking, are why I have liked myself in Spain more than I have ever liked myself before. I am less encumbered here, more receptive to experience. And more appreciative of the texture of daily life. Which includes these people. My God, look how beautiful they are, how generous and happy. And this room, with the art work, the photographs and paintings made by Chus and all of his artist friends. And the table itself. Look at this table! Plates and glasses and cups and candles and crumbs and rings of wine, the stains of consummation. My eyes close. I see my own blood, pressing against my skin, pulsing.

And later, after the second cupful, after the flush has receded, after Virginia has become bored with watching and begun to draw pictures of Papa Noel on a sketch pad belonging to Chus, after Pilar and Alberto have located the full moon over the city from the windows of the front room and described it to the rest of us who cannot move, I turn to Lola. Years later, when I have not heard from Lola for a long, long time, I will have periodic dreams about her, wild, grief-stricken dreams from which I will wake sobbing. In my subconscious she will become an emblem of loss, of what we give up when we travel, what we leave behind. But now, halfway through my year of living in her apartment, Lola simply *is*, every day.

She is thirty-three. She is beautiful. She is quiet, graceful, present. When something delights her she smiles with her whole body, and when something makes her angry or sad she speaks more quickly than I can follow. She is the connective tissue here, the person most responsible for this particular group of people coming together. From the day I moved in, after answering Lola's advertisement for a bedroom to rent—to a foreign graduate student or teacher—she has shared her friends with me.

We are shy with each other sometimes, polite and careful about the intertwining of our lives in such a small space. But at other times, after an evening with friends, Lola's friends from the newspaper or my friends from the English department, after some beer and then whiskey and then cognac, we walk along the cobbled streets of the old section of town, past the lighted cathedral, through the empty fish market, arm in arm the way Spanish women do.

Lola's best friend shares her name, so that I've taken to distinguishing them as "my Lola" and "the other Lola." When I see Pilar or Begoña on the street they sometimes say, Lola was here just minutes ago—*your* Lola.

One day months ago I came home and found my Lola sitting on the couch, pale. This was before the language got inside me, before I stopped wrestling with individual words, and although I knew that what she was telling me was very serious, I didn't understand exactly what it was. She said, "Someone called you today, a man with a very unusual name." She said, placing her hand in the middle of her chest, "Hearing that name affected me."

Now her eyes are focused on the table, but she is listening to Isabel, nodding in agreement about the problem of Papa Noel, the increasing commercialization of Christmas in this country. She sees me watching, smiles and flushes. What I understand now, now that I understand, is this: Four years ago, the love of Lola's life, a man with a very unusual name, died in a helicopter crash in the mountains outside Oviedo. He was a rescue worker, searching for a child who had wandered off a trail on a cold day. I have heard the story in bits and pieces, used my imagination to fill in the details, and mostly I force myself not to think about it because when I do I can't breathe.

I have seen photographs, heard details. They were magic together. The first time he saw her, in the university office where she was a student worker, he walked right up and kissed her full on the lips, then left without saying a word. A week later he came back, and a week after that he showed up at her apartment with a pan of chicken he had baked. He was married, and by then Lola knew it and refused to let him in. So he walked across the street to a pay phone, called her up and said, "You don't have to become involved with me, but you do have to eat this chicken because I made it for you. And you will love it."

And she did. And shortly after, he left his wife and moved in with Lola in the kind of twist that rarely happens in these situations, and for four years they were magic, until he fell out of the sky and died.

I want to ask Chus to light the fire again, to stir the flames and repeat the incantation. I want to drink again from the first cup and feel its magic, its hope, its eternal buoyancy eternally veering toward loss.

And later, after Isabel leaves with the sleepy Virginia, after the circle shrinks and we have each put on a sweater or wrapped a blanket around our shoulders in this ancient, heatless building, after the conversation has turned to work and the clock moves toward two, Chus ladles out a third helping to each of us. We clutch our lukewarm cups in both hands and raise them toward we know not what. "May the evil spirits be banished," says Chus, humming again to mock his priestly self.

It is December 21, the beginning of winter, the night of a full moon. I know that in seven days I will ride a bus to Madrid to meet the man I love, the man who is coming to visit me from New York. I know that in seven days I will hold my breath waiting to see him, and that when he leaves two weeks later I will hold my breath again, against the riskiness of this long separation. But I do not know that months later I will sit in a crowded movie theater with Lola by my side, and when a man on screen dies in a car accident, she will begin to cry and will lean over to whisper harshly that at least the man I love is alive, at least I can see him again if I choose to. And she will be right about the simplicity of things, and also wrong, and I will hold her hand until the lights come on.

In the spring that is yet to come, on a night that will be hotter than it should be, Lola and I will ride down Calle Argüelles and see Chus leaning against a dark building, pleading with a small blond woman who sobs and slaps her palms against the stone wall. Lola will slow the car until Chus looks toward us, and then she will speed up and say, "Poor Chus. Life is hard," and we will never mention it again. I will think then and always after of his face tonight, of the smile and the secrets and the way his throat moves as he hums, begging in the wordless way we all must for the spirits to be kind.

In the Subjunctive Mood

T hink of it this way: Learning to use the subjunctive mood is like learning to drive a stick shift. It's like falling in love with a car that isn't new or sporty but has a tilt steering wheel and a price you can afford. It's like being so in love with the possibilities, with the places you might go and the experiences you might have, that you pick up your new used car without quite knowing how to drive it, sputtering and stalling and rolling backward at every light. Then you drive the car each day for months, until the stalling stops and you figure out how to downshift, until you can hear the engine's registers and move through them with grace. And later, after you've gained control over the driving and lost control over so much else, you sell the car and most of your possessions and move yourself to Spain, to a place where language and circumstance will help you understand the subjunctive.

Remember that the subjunctive is a mood, not a tense. Verb tenses tell *when* something happens; moods tell *how true*. It's easy to skim over moods in a new language, to translate the words and think you've understood, which is why your first months in Spain will lack nuance. But eventually, after enough conversations have passed, enough hours of talking with your students at the University of Oviedo and your housemate, Lola, and the friends you make when you wander the streets looking like a foreigner, you'll discover that you need the subjunctive in order to finish a question, or an answer, or a thought you couldn't have had without it.

In language, as in life, moods are complicated, but at least in language there are only two. The indicative mood is for knowledge, facts, absolutes, for describing what's real or definite. You'd use the indicative to say, for example:

I was in love.

Or, *The man I loved tried to kill himself.*

Or, *I moved to Spain because the man I loved, the man who tried to kill himself, was driving me insane.*

The indicative helps you tell what happened or is happening or will happen in the future (when you believe you know for sure what the future will bring).

The subjunctive mood, on the other hand, is uncertain. It helps you tell what could have been or might be or what you want but may not get. You'd use the subjunctive to say:

I thought he'd improve without me.

Or, *I left so that he'd begin to take care of himself.*

Or later, after your perspective has been altered, by time and distance and a couple of cervezas in a brightly lit bar, you might say:

I deserted him (indicative).

I left him alone with his crazy self for a year (indicative).

Because I hoped (after which begins the subjunctive) *that being apart might allow us to come together again.*

English is losing the subjunctive mood. It lingers in some constructions ("If he *were* dead," for example), but it's no longer pervasive. That's the beauty and also the danger of English—that the definite and the might-be often look so much alike. And it's the reason why, during a period in your life when everything feels hypothetical, Spain will be a very seductive place to live.

In Spanish, verbs change to accommodate the subjunctive in every tense, and the rules, which are many and varied, have exceptions. In the beginning you may feel defeated by this, even hopeless and angry sometimes. But eventually, in spite of your frustration with trying to explain, you'll know in the part of your mind that holds your stories, the part where grammar is felt before it's understood, that the uses of the subjunctive matter.

1. with "Ojalá"

Ojalá means *I hope* or, more literally, *that Allah is willing.* It's one of the many words left over from the Moorish occupation of Spain, one that's followed by the subjunctive mood because, of course, you never know for sure what Allah has in mind.

During the first months in Spain, you'll use the word by itself, a kind of dangling wish. "It's supposed to rain," Lola will say, and you'll respond, "Ojalá." You'll know you're confusing her, leaving her to figure out whether you want the rain or not, but sometimes the mistakes are too hard to bear. "That Allah is willing it wouldn't have raining," you might accidentally say. And besides, so early into this year of living freely, you're not quite sure what to hope for.

Each time you say *Ojalá*, it will feel like a prayer, the "ja" and "la" like breaths, like faith woven right into the language. It will remind you of La Mezquita, the enormous, graceful mosque in Córdoba. Of being eighteen years old and visiting Spain for the first time, how you stood in the courtyard filled with orange trees, trying to admire the building before you. You had a fever then, a summer virus you hadn't yet recognized because it was so hot outside. Too hot to lift a hand to fan your face. Too hot to wonder why your head throbbed and the world spun slowly around you.

Inside, the darkness felt like cool water covering your eyes, such contrast, such relief. And then the pillars began to emerge, rows and rows of pillars supporting red and white brick arches, a massive stone ceiling balanced above them like a thought. You swam behind the guide, not even trying to understand his words but soothed by the vastness, by the shadows. Each time you felt dizzy you looked up toward the arches, the floating stone. Toward something that felt, you realized uncomfortably, like God. Or Allah. Or whatever force inspired people to defy gravity this way.

Later, after ten years have passed, after you've moved to Oviedo and become fascinated with the contours of language, the man you left behind in New York will come to visit. You'll travel south with him, returning to La Mezquita on a January afternoon when the air is mild and the orange trees wave tiny green fruit. He'll carry the guidebook, checking it periodically to get the history straight, while you try to reconcile the place before you with the place in your memory, comparing the shadows of this low sun with the light of another season.

You'll be here because you want this man to see La Mezquita. You want him to feel the mystery of a darkness that amazes and consoles, that makes you feel the presence in empty spaces of something you can't explain. Approaching the shadow of the door, you'll each untie the sweaters from around your waists, slipping your arms into them and then into each other's. He will squint and you will hold your breath. *Ojalá*, you'll think, glimpsing in the shadows the subjunctive mood at work.

2. after words of suasion and negation

In Oviedo, you'll become a swimmer. Can you imagine? Two or three times a week you'll pack a bag and walk for thirty-five minutes to the university pool, where you'll place clothes and contact lenses in a locker, then sink into a crowded lane. The pool is a mass of blurry heads and arms, some of which know what they're doing and most of which, like you, are flailing. You keep bumping into people as you make your way from one end of the pool to the other, but no one gets upset, and you reason that any form of motion equals exercise.

Then one day a miracle happens. You notice the guy in the next lane swimming like a pro, his long arms cutting ahead as he glides, rhythmically, stroke-stroke-breath. You see and hear and feel the rhythm, and before long you're following him, stroking when he strokes, breathing when he breathes. He keeps getting away, swimming three laps to your one, so you wait at the edge of the pool for him to come back, then follow again, practicing. At the end of an hour, you realize that this man you don't know, a man you wouldn't recognize clothed, has taught you to swim. To breathe. To use the water instead of fighting against it. For this alone, you'll later say, it was worth moving to Spain.

Stroke-stroke-breath becomes the rhythm of your days, the rhythm of your life in Oviedo. All through the fall months, missing him the way you'd miss a limb, your muscles strain to create distance. Shallow end to deep end and back, you're swimming away. From memories of abrupt mood shifts. From the way a question, a comment, a person walking past a restaurant window could transform him into a hunched-over man wearing anger like a shawl. From the echo of your own voice trying to be patient and calm, saying, *Listen to me. I want you to call the doctor.* In English you said *listen* and *call,* and they were the same words you'd use to relate a fact instead of make a plea. But in Spanish, in the language that fills your mind as you swim continually away, the moment you try to persuade someone, or dissuade, you enter the realm of the subjunctive. The verb ends differently so there can be no mistake: requesting is not at all the same as getting.

3. with "si" or "como si"

Si means *if*. *Como si* means *as if*. A clause that begins with *si* or *como si* is followed by the subjunctive when the meaning is hypothetical or contrary to fact. For example:

If I'd known he would harm himself, I wouldn't have left him alone.

But here we have to think about whether the if-clause really is contrary to fact. Two days before, you'd asked him what he felt like doing that night and he'd responded, "I feel like jumping off the Mid-Hudson Bridge." He'd looked serious when he said it, and even so you'd replied, "Really? Would you like me to drive you there?" *As if* it were a joke.

If you knew he were serious, that he were thinking of taking his life, would you have replied with such sarcasm? In retrospect it seems impossible not to have known—the classic signs were there. For weeks he'd been sad, self-pitying. He'd been sleeping too much, getting up to teach his Freshman Composition class in the morning, then going home some days and staying in bed until evening. His sense of humor had waned. He'd begun asking the people around him to cheer him up, make him feel better, please.

And yet he'd been funny. Ironic, self-deprecating, hyperbolic. So no one's saying you should have known, just that maybe you felt a hint of threat in his statement about the river. And maybe that angered you because it meant you were failing to be enough for him. Maybe you were tired, too, in need of cheering up yourself because suddenly your perfect guy had turned inside out. Or maybe that realization came later, after you'd had the time and space to develop theories.

The truth is, only you know what you know. And what you know takes the indicative, remember?

For example: You knew he was hurting himself. The moment you saw the note on his office door, in the campus building where you were supposed to meet him on a Sunday afternoon, you knew. The note said, "I'm not feeling well. I'm going home. I guess I'll see you tomorrow." He didn't use your name.

You tried calling him several times but there was no answer, so you drove to the apartment he shared with another graduate student. The front door was unlocked, but his bedroom door wouldn't budge. You knocked steadily but not too loud, because his housemate's bedroom door was also closed, and you assumed he was inside taking a nap. *If* you'd known that his housemate was not actually home, you would have broken down the door. That scenario is hypothetical, so it takes the subjunctive—even though you're quite sure.

The human mind can reason its way around anything. On the drive to your own apartment, you told yourself, he's angry with me. That's why the door was locked, why he wouldn't answer the phone. You thought: If he weren't so close to his family, I'd really be worried. If today weren't Mother's Day. If he didn't talk so affectionately about his parents. About his brother and sisters. About our future. If, if, if.

When the phone rang and there was silence on the other end, you began to shout, "What have you done?"

In Spain, late at night over chupitos of bourbon or brandy, you and Lola will trade stories. Early on you won't understand a lot of what she says, and she'll understand what you say but not what you mean. You won't know how to say what you mean in Spanish; sometimes you won't even know how to say it in English. But as time goes on, the stories you tell will become more complicated. More subtle. More grammatically daring. You'll begin to feel more at ease in the unreal.

For example: *If* you hadn't gone straight home from his apartment. *If* you hadn't answered the phone. *If* you hadn't jumped back into your car to drive nine miles in record time, hoping the whole way to be stopped by the police. *If* you hadn't met him on the porch where he had staggered in blood-soaked clothes. *If* you hadn't rushed upstairs for a towel and discovered a flooded bedroom floor, the blood separating into water and rust-colored clumps. *If* you hadn't been available for this emergency.

As the months pass in Spain, you'll begin to risk the *then*. His housemate would have come home and found him the way you found him: deep gashes in his arm, but the wounds clotting enough to keep him alive, enough to narrowly avoid a transfusion. His housemate would have called the paramedics, ridden to the hospital in the ambulance, notified his parents from the emergency room, greeted them after their three-hour drive. His housemate would have done all the things you did, and he would have cleaned the mess by himself instead of with your help, the two of you borrowing a neighbor's wet-vac and working diligently until you—or he—or both of you—burst into hysterical laughter. Later this housemate would have moved to a new apartment, just as he has done, and would probably be no worse off than he is right now.

You, on the other hand, would have felt ashamed, guilty, remiss for not being available in a time of crisis. But you wouldn't have found yourself leaning over a stretcher in the emergency room, a promise slipping from your mouth before you could think it through: "I won't leave you. Don't worry, I won't leave you." *As if* it were true.

4. after impersonal expressions

Such as *it is possible, it is a shame, it is absurd.*

"*It's possible* that I'm making things worse in some ways," you told the counselor you saw on Thursday afternoons. He'd been out of the hospital for a few months by then and had a habit of missing his therapy appointments, to which you could only respond by signing up for your own.

She asked how you were making things worse, and you explained that when you told him you needed to be alone for a night and he showed up anyway at 11:00 PM, pleading to stay over, you couldn't turn him away. She said, "*It's a shame* he won't honor your request," and you pressed your fingernails into the flesh of your palm to keep your eyes from filling. She asked why you didn't want him to stay over, and you said that sometimes you just wanted to sleep, without waking up when he went to the bathroom and listening to make sure he came back to bed instead of taking all the Tylenol in the medicine cabinet. Or sticking his head in the gas oven. Or diving from the balcony onto the hillside three stories below. There is nothing, you told her, nothing I haven't thought of.

She said, "Do you think he's manipulating you?" and you answered in the mood of certainty, "Yes. Absolutely." Then you asked, "*Isn't it absurd* that I let him manipulate me?" and what you wanted, of course, was some reassurance that it wasn't absurd. That you were a normal person, reacting in a normal way, to a crazy situation.

Instead she said, "Let's talk about why you let him. Let's talk about what's in this for you."

5. after verbs of doubt or emotion

You didn't think he was much of a prospect at first. Because he seemed arrogant. Because in the initial meetings for new instructors, he talked as if he were doing it the right way and the rest of you were pushovers. Because he looked at you with one eye squinted, as if he couldn't quite decide.

You liked that he was funny, a little theatrical and a great fan of supermarkets. At 10:00 PM, after evening classes ended, he'd say, "Are you going home?" Sometimes you'd offer to drop him off at his place. Sometimes you'd agree to go out for a beer. And sometimes you'd say, "Yeah, but I have to go to the store first," and his eyes would light up. In the supermarket he'd push the cart and you'd pick items off the shelf. Maybe you'd turn around and there would be a whole rack of frozen ribs in your cart, or after you put them back, three boxes of Lucky Charms. Maybe he'd be holding a package of pfeffernusse and telling a story about his German grandmother. Maybe it would take two hours to run your errand because he was courting you in ShopRite.

You doubted that you'd sleep with him a second time. After the first time, you both lay very still for a while, flat on your backs, not touching. He seemed to be asleep. You watched the digital clock hit 2:30 AM and thought about finding your turtleneck and sweater and wool socks, lacing up your boots, and heading out into the snow. And then out of the blue he rolled toward you, pulled the blanket up around your shoulders, and said, "Is there anything I can get you? A cup of tea? A sandwich?"

You were thrilled at the breaks in his depression, breaks that felt like new beginnings, every time. Days, sometimes even weeks, when he seemed more like himself than ever before. Friends would ask how he was doing, and he'd offer a genuine smile. "Much better," he'd say, putting his arm around you, "She's pulling me through the death-wish phase." Everyone would laugh with relief, and at those moments you'd feel luckier than ever before, because of the contrast.

Do you see the pattern?

6. to express good wishes

Que tengas muy buen viaje, Lola will say, kissing each of your cheeks before leaving you off at the bus station. *May you have a good trip.* A hope, a wish, a prayer of sorts, even without the *Ojalá*.

The bus ride from Oviedo to Madrid is nearly six hours, so you have a lot of time for imagining. It's two days after Christmas, and you know he spent the holiday at his parents' house, that he's there right now, maybe eating breakfast, maybe packing. Tonight his father will drive him to Kennedy Airport, and tomorrow morning, very early, you'll meet him at Barajas in Madrid. You try to envision what he'll look like, the expression on his face when he sees you, but you're having trouble recalling what it's like to be in his presence.

You try not to hope too much, although now, four months into your life in Spain, you want to move toward, instead of away. Toward long drives on winding, mountain roads, toward the cathedral of Toledo, the mosque at Córdoba, the Alhambra in Granada. Toward romantic dinners along the Mediterranean. Toward a new place from which to view the increasingly distant past. You want this trip to create a separation, in your mind and in his, between your first relationship and your real relationship, the one that will be so wonderful, so stable, you'll never leave him again.

Once you've reached Madrid and found the pensión where you've reserved a room, you'll get the innkeeper to help you make an international call. His father will say, "My God, he can't sit still today," and then there will be his voice, asking how your bus ride was, where you are, how far from the airport. You'll say, "I'll see you in the morning." He'll reply, "In seventeen hours."

The next morning, the taxi driver is chatty. He wants to know why you're going to the airport without luggage, and your voice is happy and excited when you explain. He asks whether this boyfriend writes you letters, and you smile and nod at the reflection in the rearview mirror. "Many letters?" he continues, "Do you enjoy receiving the letters?" In Spain you're always having odd conversations with strangers, so you hesitate only a moment, wondering why he cares, and then you say, "Yes. Very much." He nods emphatically. "Muy bien." At the terminal he drops you off with a broad smile. "Que lo pases bien con tu novio," he says. *Have a good time with your boyfriend.* In his words you hear the requisite subjunctive mood.

7. in adverbial clauses denoting purpose, provision, exception

How different to walk down the street in Madrid, Toledo, Córdoba, to notice an elaborate fountain or a tiny car parked half on the sidewalk, and comment aloud. You've loved being alone in Spain and now, even more, you love being paired.

On the fifth day you reach Granada, find lodging in someone's home. Down the hallway you can hear the family watching TV, cooking, preparing to celebrate New Year's Eve. In the afternoon you climb the long, slow hill leading to the Alhambra and spend hours touring the complex. You marvel at the elaborate irrigation system, the indoor baths with running water, the stunning mosaic tiles and views of the Sierra Nevada. Here is the room where Boabdil signed the city's surrender to Ferdinand and Isabella; here is where Washington Irving lived while writing *Tales of the Alhambra*. Occasionally you separate, as he inspects a mural and you follow a hallway into a lush courtyard, each of your imaginations working to restore this place to its original splendor. When you come together again, every time, there's a thrill.

He looks rested, relaxed, strolling through the gardens with his hands tucked into the front pockets of his pants. When you enter the Patio of the Lions—the famous courtyard where a circle of marble lions project water into a reflecting pool—he turns to you, wide-eyed, his face as open as a boy's.

"Isn't it pretty?" you keep asking, feeling shy because what you mean is: "Are you glad to be here?"

"*So* pretty," he responds, taking hold of your arm, touching his lips to your hair.

The day is perfect, you think. The trip is perfect. You allow yourself a moment of triumph: I left him *so that* he would get better without me, and he did. I worked hard and saved money and invited him on this trip *in case* there's still hope for us. And there is.

Unless. In language, as in experience, we have purpose, provision, exception. None of which necessarily matches reality, and all of which take the subjunctive.

On the long walk back down the hill toward your room, he turns quiet. You find yourself talking more than usual, trying to fill the empty space with cheerful commentary, but it doesn't help. The shape of his face begins to change until there it is again, that landscape of furrows and crags. The jaw thrusts slightly, lips pucker, eyebrows arch as if to say, "I don't care. About anything."

Back in the room, you ask him what's wrong, plead with him to tell you. You can talk about anything, you assure him, anything at all. And yet you're stunned when his brooding turns accusatory. He says it isn't fair. You don't understand how difficult it is to be him. Your life is easy, so easy that even moving to a new country, taking up a new language, is effortless. While every day is a struggle for him. Don't you see that? Every day is a struggle.

He lowers the window shade and gets into bed, his back turned toward you.

What to do? You want to go back outside into the mild air and sunshine, walk until you remember what it feels like to be completely alone. But you're afraid to leave him. For the duration of his ninety-minute nap, you sit paralyzed. Everything feels unreal, the darkened room, the squeals of children in another part of the house, the burning sensation in your stomach. You tremble, first with sadness and fear, then with anger. Part of you wants to wake him, tell him to collect his things, then drive him back to the airport in Madrid. You want to send him home again, away from your new country, the place where you live unencumbered—but with a good deal of effort, thank you. The other part of you wants to wail, to beat your fists against the wall and howl, *Give him back to me.*

Remember: purpose, provision, exception. The subjunctive runs parallel to reality.

8. after certain indications of time, if the action has not occurred

While is a subjunctive state of mind. So are *until, as soon as, before,* and *after.* By now you understand why, right? Because until something *has happened,* you can't be sure.

In Tarifa, the wind blows and blows. You learn this even before arriving, as you drive down Route 15 past Gibraltar. You're heading toward the southern-most point in Spain, toward warm sea breezes and a small town off the beaten path. You drive confidently, shifting quickly through the gears to keep pace with the traffic around you. He reclines in the passenger's seat, one foot propped against the dashboard, reading from the *Real Guide* open against his thigh. "Spreading out beyond its Moorish walls, Tarifa is known in Spain for its abnormally high suicide rate—a result of the unremitting winds that blow across the town and its environs."

You say, "Tell me you're joking." He says, "How's that for luck?"

Three days before, you'd stood in Granada's crowded city square at midnight, each eating a grape for every stroke of the New Year. If you eat all twelve grapes in time, tradition says, you'll have plenty of luck in the coming year. It sounds wonderful—such an easy way to secure good fortune—until you start eating and time gets ahead, so far ahead that no matter how fast you chew and swallow, midnight sounds with three grapes left.

In Tarifa, you come down with the flu. It hits hard and fast—one minute you're strolling through a white-washed coastal town, and the next you're huddled in bed in a stupor. He goes to the pharmacy and, with a handful of Spanish words and many gestures, procures the right medicine. You sleep all day, through the midday meal, through the time of siesta, past sundown, and into the evening. When you wake the room is fuzzy and you're alone, with a vague memory of him rubbing your back, saying something about a movie.

Carefully you rise and make your way to the bathroom—holding onto the bed, the doorway, the sink—then stand on your toes and look out the window into the blackness. By day there's a thin line of blue mountains across the strait, and you imagine catching the ferry at dawn and watching that sliver of Morocco rise up from the shadows to become a whole continent. You imagine standing on the other side and looking back toward the tip of Spain, this tiny town where the winds blow and blow. That's how easy it is to keep traveling once you start, putting distance between the various parts of your life, imagining yourself over and over again into entirely new places.

Chilly and sweating, you make your way back to bed, your stomach fluttering nervously. You think back to Granada, how he'd woken from a nap on that dark afternoon and apologized. "I don't know what got into me today," he'd said. "This hasn't been happening." You believe it's true, it hasn't been happening. But you don't know *how true*.

You think: He's fine now. There's no need to worry. He's been fine for days, happy and calm. I'm overreacting. But overreaction is a slippery slope. With the wind howling continuously outside, the room feels small and isolated. You don't know that he's happy and calm right now, do you? You don't know how he is today at all, because you've slept and slept and barely talked to him.

You think: If the movie started on time—but movies never start on time in Spain, so you add, subtract, try to play it safe, and determine that by 10:45 PM your fretting will be justified. At 11:00 PM you'll get dressed and go looking, and if you can't find him, what will you do? Wait until midnight for extra measure? And then call the police? And tell them what, that he isn't back yet, and you're afraid because you're sick and he's alone and the wind here blows and blows, enough to make people crazy, the book says, make them suicidal?

This is the *when*, the *while*, the *until*. The *before* and *after*. The real and the unreal in precarious balance. This is what you moved to Spain to escape from, and here it is again, following you.

The next time you wake, the room seems brighter, more familiar. You sit up and squint against the light. His cheeks are flushed, hair mussed from the wind. His eyes are clear as a morning sky. "Hi, sweetie," he says, putting a hand on your forehead. "You still have a fever. How do you feel?" He smells a little musty, like the inside of a community theater where not many people go on a Sunday night in early January. He says, "The movie was hilarious." You ask whether he understood it and he shrugs. Then he acts out a scene using random Spanish words as a voice-over, and you laugh and cough until he flops down on his stomach beside you.

Here it comes again, the contrast between what was, just a little while ago, and what is now. After all this time and all these miles, you're both here, in a Spanish town with a view of Africa. You feel amazed, dizzy, as if swimming outside yourself. You're talking with him, but you're also watching yourself talk with him. And then you're sleeping and watching yourself sleep, dreaming and thinking about the dreams. Throughout the night you move back and forth, here and there, between what is and what might be, tossed by language and possibility and the constantly shifting wind.

9. in certain independent clauses

There's something extraordinary—isn't there?—about learning to speak Spanish as an adult, about coming to see grammar as a set of guidelines not just for saying what you mean but for understanding the way you live. There's something extraordinary about thinking in a language that insists on marking the limited power of desire.

For example: At Barajas Airport in Madrid, you walk him to the boarding gate. He turns to face you, hands on your arms, eyes green as the sea. He says, "Only a few more months and we'll be together for good, right sweetie?" He watches your face, waiting for a response, but you know this isn't a decision, something you can say yes to. So you smile, eyes burning, and give a slight nod. What you mean is, *I hope so.* What you think is, *Ojalá.* And what you know is this: The subjunctive is the mood of mystery. Of luck. Of faith interwoven with doubt. It's a held breath, a hand reaching out, carefully touching wood. It's humility, deference, the opposite of hubris. And it's going to take a long time to master.

But at least the final rule of usage is simple, self-contained, one you can commit to memory: Certain independent clauses exist only in the subjunctive mood, lacing optimism with resignation, hope with heartache. *Be that as it may*, for example. Or the phrase one says at parting, eyes closed as if in prayer, *May all go well with you.*

Having Hunger

am hungry, we say in English, using an adjective to describe a state of being that momentarily defines us. But in Spanish one uses a noun, as if naming a possession, a visitation, a tide of physical yearning. *Tengo hambre*: I have hunger. Either way, of course, the stomach gurgles and pangs, the body's needs engage the mind, which loiters and obsesses. And yet language matters. The hunger of *tengo hambre* is a different hunger than I'm used to. This hunger doesn't define or describe me, it names the thing I'm struggling against. In Spanish, in Spain, in a place I love for a time that is temporary, hunger sometimes nearly undoes me.

This weekend is one of those times. Riding in the back seat of Yolanda and José's car, my arms quiver and my brain feels like it's swathed in gauze. Partly this is from the motion sickness medicine I took before we left Oviedo, the non-drowsy formula that offers a pleasant buzz. But the hunger goes beyond that, coming from a place I can't locate. On the seat beside me is a large, square box of marzipan cookies, a gift for Yolanda's parents that is begging to be opened. I imagine sliding a fingernail beneath the corner of its cellophane wrapper, hearing the crinkle as it tears, feeling the suctioned resistance of the box top prying loose from its mate. Inside, beneath a thin layer of waxed paper, the golden cookies lie in a dark brown tray. I want to pick them up one by one, suck their rich sweetness against the roof of my mouth, chew and swallow until the entire box is empty and the trembling in my limbs subsides.

Outside the car window, the landscape has shifted from the green mountains of Asturias to the rolling, arid province of León. I'm astonished by the stark beauty of the colors: rust, ginger, the palest of green against a cobalt sky. Or rather, I would be astonished if my senses weren't so muted. At one point José slows down and points out a goat tethered to the pole of a speed limit sign, gnawing at some grass. "He's been abandoned," José says, and I want to muster concern for the animal, but all I can focus on is the reach of its neck, the motion in its jaw. A small tavern appears up ahead, and Yolanda declares the mystery solved: the goat's owner must have needed some refreshment.

We're on our way to a tiny farming community that consists, I've been warned, of one church and two bars. I'm excited to get away from the city, to meet Yolanda's parents and spend time in a region of Spain I haven't yet visited. But I'm also nervous. Oviedo has become such a comfortable place that sometimes, wrapped up in the concerns of daily life, I forget I'm a foreigner there. In a small village, with a new regional accent to decode and people who aren't accustomed to my faulty Spanish, I know I'll be anxious about my outsider status and worried that my behavior may seem tied to my nationality. I'm continually struck by the easy connections Europeans draw between individuals and the culture they're from. "The French prefer to . . ." or "People in Switzerland don't . . ." The comments aren't derogatory, they're simply observations in a place where heritage matters, as does generalizing about the world in which we live. And yet all of this has made me self-conscious. I'm aware that people's interactions with me may be colored by assumptions about the United States and that my own behavior—my social missteps and moments of naiveté—might seem decidedly American.

When José finally stops the car in front of a modest, two-story home, we unfold ourselves into the middle of a very warm Saturday. It's early March, and the temperature seems incongruous with the landscape. The grass is brownish-green, the sun flows unimpeded through the leafless trees scattered along the road. We all squint and yawn and stretch, trying to come to life as Yolanda's mother appears at the front door. "Buenos días!" she calls, smoothing her skirt with one hand and her hair with the other, perhaps more nervous than I am. Before Yolanda can introduce us, her mother says, "¡La Americana!" and steps forward to kiss each of my cheeks. Then she cocks her head to one side and asks, "You really don't eat meat? Not even steak? I thought Americans loved steak."

I take her disbelief as a compliment. It's true that I don't eat meat, although I've added both fish and chicken to my diet since moving to Spain. I've also gotten used to asking up front whether a dish contains *carne* and being told emphatically "No, no," only to find bits of ham or bacon peering out of it. It isn't that I'm being lied to, it's that the people who serve these meals can't imagine that by *meat* I mean the tiny flecks of cured pork that give all the flavor to a plate of beans. Their way of thinking makes more sense than mine. I have a hard time explaining my diet, even to myself. I don't eat this way for ethical or political reasons, and while I had health in mind when I turned to vegetarianism years ago, one could argue that a love of salt and sugar is more dangerous than the occasional hamburger. Nonetheless, it's true that here in Spain, my avoidance of meat makes me feel less like an excessive American.

Today, however, that's exactly what I am—excessive, insatiable. Inside the house, the aroma of sautéed garlic weakens my knees. We climb a flight of stairs into a large hallway, from which I can see the kitchen, its pots and pans steaming on the stove. Yolanda's father appears, kissing my cheeks and asking about the drive. I offer him my gift, then experience an intense moment of longing when he accepts the box of cookies and carries it away.

While Yolanda helps her mother in the kitchen, José leads me on a tour of the house, his words competing for my attention with sounds from the kitchen: the ceramic bumping of dishes, an oven opening and closing. In the living room, the hallway, and the room where I'll sleep in a neatly made twin bed, José points out landscape paintings that Yolanda's mother has made. They're beautifully rendered scenes like the ones we drove through as we neared this town: stretches of auburn land, thin forests of oak and poplar trees, a reservoir so brilliantly blue that the painting would seem absurd if I hadn't witnessed that very scene half an hour ago. I have the urge to slip inside the paintings, to gather wild strawberries from that hillside, fish in the reservoir, make a delicious meal of everything I see. It's a crazy impulse, the kind of thinking that comes with a high fever. I place the back of my hand against my neck and breathe deeply, trying to bring myself under control.

Yolanda's parents have already eaten, and there's a feast left over. Chicken in white wine, boiled potatoes with parsley and mayonnaise, asparagus, crusty bread, and for dessert sections of pineapple and cantaloupe. By the time we sit down at the table, I'm ravenous. I try to eat slowly, to savor the tastes and textures, when what I really want is to take huge, rapid forkfuls, chew with my mouth open, go back for more, again and again. It's a bestial impulse that fills me with shame. I put my fork down between bites, count the number of times I chew before swallowing, but there's some pure desire at my core that threatens to overpower me. I monitor Yolanda's and José's plates, gauging my progress against theirs, trying not to finish first. *Stop it*, I say to myself, but I can't. I feel bewitched, possessed, transformed into someone I almost don't recognize.

Like many Americans, I have a complex relationship with food. Although I've never gone a day without enough to eat, it's as if I've inherited the fear of scarcity on a genetic level. When I was growing up, adults regularly exhorted kids to clean their plates because people were starving in China, as if consumption were the ethical response to prosperity. At the same time the refrain "You are what you eat" cautioned against excess. Like many people I know, I developed binge-and-regret habits very early on. Even as an adult, I struggle with this pattern. For a period of time I'll eat too much of foods I know are unhealthy—French fries, muffins, ice cream—as if fattening up for some future shortage. And of course the shortage comes as I deprive myself for weeks or months, trying to undo the damage. It's a way of being that disturbs me greatly, that seems immature at best and neurotic at worst. And it's one of the things I've hoped to change during my time in Spain.

I became aware of the desperate need for change soon after arriving in Oviedo, during the first midday meal with my housemate. We had agreed to cook separately because of my meat issues, and on that day I'd made stir-fried vegetables and rice. We sat down to eat at the same time, 2:30 in the afternoon, Lola with her first course and me with my colorful plate. I'd eaten breakfast at 9:00 in the morning, and as far as my body was concerned starvation was imminent, so I dug in, polishing off the entire meal in the time it took Lola to finish her soup. When she noticed that I was sitting back, sated, she couldn't hide her disgust. "Don't Americans care to taste their food?" she asked.

Since then, I've paid special attention to meals, clearing time and space in the day for nourishment. In my previous life, lunch meant eating a sandwich at my desk or while driving in the car, paying little attention to what I was doing. Here, *la comida* means a tablecloth, a meal of at least two courses followed by a piece of fruit and coffee or tea. It means an hour at the table, digesting not just the meal but the day that's in progress. As ingrained as it still is for me to think of lunch around noon or 1:00 PM, I've grown to appreciate the Spanish rhythm and to feel healthier because of it.

But sometimes, late on a Friday afternoon when Lola has gone to work and I have no plans for the evening, I find my old ways creeping back. Like an addict, I skulk down to the market and buy a giant chocolate bar laced with nuts and raisins, the kind that contains a dozen servings. Then I return to the apartment and switch on the television, sunlight slanting into the living room window so beautifully that I ache with loneliness. I sit on Lola's maroon couch and eat one thick square at a time, feeling tremendously comforted by the sensation of chewing and swallowing, by the velvety chocolate coating my throat, by the connection to a part of myself that's come out of hiding. Less than two hours after a big meal, I'll eat the entire bar, square by square, amazed at my capacity for ingestion. Afterwards I'll feel horrified, angry with myself for such overindulgence, and I'll put the wrapper in my purse, not wanting Lola to see it in the trash. At the same time, part of me will savor the memory of eating, the glorious pleasure of excess.

We all have a gluttonous part of ourselves that needs placating from time to time, of course. But for reasons I don't yet understand, traveling to the region of León this weekend has provoked that part of me until it threatens to burst forth and reveal itself to the world. I tell myself it's just the motion sickness pill, that it's lowered my blood sugar making me feel hungrier than usual. But I don't really believe this. The medicine has never affected me this way in the past, and now that I've had a full meal, my hands have stopped trembling and the hollow feeling in my legs is gone. But still I want to eat. I fantasize about a room filled with food, buffet tables piled high with every kind of fish and cheese and cake and no one around, absolutely no one but me, and I can eat until it's physically impossible to eat any more.

When the last piece of fruit has disappeared from the bowl and our wine glasses are empty, I feel bereft. José suggests driving to the nearest city, Astorga, where we can go for a walk and visit some historic sites. I think that's a good idea—anything, really, to distract me from this hunger. Then Yolanda smiles impishly and suggests that before we leave, why not try out the cookies I brought? "Just to make sure they're good enough for my parents," she winks, and I feel too grateful to speak.

Yolanda and I became friends not long after I arrived in Spain, when she hired me to help translate into English an article she'd written as part of her doctoral work in Psychology. I immediately liked her wry sense of humor and whimsical style, the tailored batik blouses she wore, the bright blue sneakers with purple laces, and the mass of short curls that sprung from her head. A couple of weeks after we finished the work, Yolanda invited me to have a drink with her and her boyfriend. José's somber expression intimidated me at first, but I quickly discovered that, like Yolanda, he was funny, intellectually curious, and patient with my language skills.

Since then we've followed a pattern of almost weekly dates, and because Yolanda and José both want to improve their English, we divide our conversations between the two languages, correcting each other and explaining grammar and usage. Often we arrive at a café with lists of questions, from slang expressions we don't understand to cultural confusions. "Why is New York City called the Big Apple?" José asked one evening. When I confessed I had no idea, Yolanda said she always assumed it was because there are so many blocks in New York. I was baffled until she explained that the Spanish word for apple, *manzana*, is also the word for city block.

So often learning a new language feels like skating on a frozen pond, whirling atop a whole body of water I want to swim in. Signs of progress are frustratingly slow, but the hours I spend with Yolanda and José, chatting through coffee or beer or, in the early morning hours, small glasses of whiskey, offer a sense of hope to which I've become addicted. I've internalized the rhythmic spacing of our meetings so that if I haven't seen them for ten days, I wake up in the morning craving their conversation. This, too, is a kind of hunger, part of the compendium of desires that grows out of living in a temporary way, in a place that is both increasingly familiar and persistently foreign.

I've internalized other rhythms, too, that give texture to this time. My teaching job provides a routine, my students a sense of constant familiarity, and I've developed periodic cravings for the seashore thirty kilometers away or the meditative calm of the Campoamor Theatre just before a performance begins. Part of being alone in a new culture involves anchoring the self with repetitions that create a sense of personal history. In that regard, my hungers are different here than they've ever been before. I'm in consumption mode always, trying to take in, to memorize, to sink down in a way that involves living fully, even for a short while.

By the time we tuck ourselves back into the car, my medicinal buzz has worn off. As José speeds along the country road, I peer through the rear window, marveling that we've moved so quickly today between contrasting landscapes. Oviedo is surrounded by the lush farmland of Asturias. The predominant color of that region is green, in every shade imaginable, while here in León the soil, the houses, the municipal buildings we pass all belong to an earthy spectrum of yellow-red-brown. Undulating hills and plowed fields gape skyward, toward the rain that hasn't come in a very long time, and I feel drawn to the muted beauty of this countryside, to its perpetual yearning.

We stop in the village of Castrillo de los Polvazares, where all the buildings were constructed in the seventeenth century from ferrous stone. A warm orange tint emanates from the low houses, the church, the wall encircling the village, and contrasts with the bright green paint on doors and window trim. As we stroll through the streets, the dusty, russet earth coats our shoes. When an orange sun breaks through some clouds in the west, everything—the wall, the cobblestone path, the soil—seems to glow. The lighting is surreal, almost alarming in its temporality, and I have the urge to reach out and take hold of someone's hand, to ground myself with touch.

Yolanda and José walk along, leaning slightly into each other. I admire their interactions, their stability, and I yearn for the physicality of being coupled. It's been two months since my boyfriend came from New York to visit me, and what I miss most is the impromptu, unselfconscious touching—not in the way I've grown accustomed to in this very demonstrative culture but in a more insistent, more proprietary sense. With a friend, the hand makes contact—pressing, resting—as a point of emphasis in one particular moment. With a romantic partner, the touch echoes not only this moment but last night, yesterday morning, the week before; it's a parallel conversation in which the past infuses the present, anticipating the future. I miss everything about that.

At the same time, I'm thankful for the relationships that being here alone has helped me develop. Yolanda, José, and I have spent many hours trading stories, narrating experiences from the parts of our lives that don't intersect. There's an intimacy growing between us, an affectionate connection that goes beyond accidents of time and circumstance. I have the sense that if I'd met these two anywhere else, at any other time, we would have fallen into a friendship. If we'd all been pilgrims, for example, walking the route from France, through the Pyrenees, across Navarra, La Rioja, Castilla on our way to pay homage in Santiago de Compostela, we would have risen early one morning in the capital city of León, walked the first kilometers west in silence as our stiff muscles adapted to motion once again, then resumed our conversations about language and culture. We would have shared even then an appreciation for irony and absurdity, and we would have arrived that evening in the next city along the route, filled with fatigue and the kind of deep-seated psychic hunger that travel often brings.

In Astorga, where more than twenty-five inns once catered to medieval pilgrims on their way to Santiago, the streets are lined with cafés that call out to me. The smell of sautéed onions beckons from open doors, and even the smoked hams hanging by twine in the windows appeal to me. Suddenly I can't believe I don't eat meat. What kind of sense does that make? If I had a ham hock in front of me this minute, I believe I would gnaw the meat straight off the bone.

I know that my hunger is unreasonable, that there's no possible way my digestive system is sending out signals of distress. This hunger comes from the brain, from the central nervous system, from mild psychosis — who knows? I don't need food. But I crave the delicious pleasure of biting, chewing, swallowing, taking into my body more and more of the physical world around me. Honestly, I think as I breathe deeply and exhale slowly, I'm having some kind of a fit.

We walk to the Plaza del Ayuntamiento, where the baroque city hall commands everyone's attention. José points out the clock tower flanked by two wooden puppets in regional costume, their mallets poised to strike a bell. Although it's ten past the hour now, so many tourists are gathered in the square that we wait a little while, hoping vainly for a display. Then we continue on, taking in the atmosphere of the small city, the humid breeze, the visitors like us strolling and pointing. We come upon the gothic cathedral, illuminated against the dusky sky, and beside it the garish Bishop's Palace, designed by Gaudí at the end of the nineteenth century. I'm sorry to learn that the palace is already closed for the day. I would have liked to roam through it—anything, really, to take my mind off this singular obsession. "No tengo hambre," I repeat under my breath as we walk, and each time my mind goes toward food, I give a quick, sharp pinch to my thigh. I don't have hunger this weekend; it has me.

At 11:00 PM, the time we'd be getting ready to go out on a Saturday night in Oviedo, we return to the house exhausted. Because it's too early for bed, we sit on the second-floor deck off the kitchen and admire the moon. It's nearly full, illuminating the outlines of trees, rooftops, a ridge in the distance. Over pizza in Astorga—thick, yeasty dough with a spicy tomato sauce and goat cheese, washed down with a large glass of beer that did, for a blissful moment, fill me up—we had talked about the clear sky tonight. José mentioned that Saturn might be visible in the west this weekend, and Yolanda described the telescope she'd given him at Christmas, which they keep at her parents' house. Now, exhilarated by the scene before me, the expanse of sky and the romance of being here, I ask if we can't set up the telescope, have a look at the cosmos.

It's a cliché to describe travel as romantic, but as with most clichés, there's truth at its core. For me, the romance of Spain comes not from idealizing the place or the people but from feeling constantly courted. Invitations come to me all the time, from friends, colleagues, students, acquaintances. Every week someone asks me to go, to see, to take in. I tour fishing villages on the coast, hike in the spectacular Picos de Europa. I'm invited into homes, introduced to families, presented with superior wines and regional specialties. At first I felt shy, undeserving in the face of all this generosity, but eventually I realized that we are all ambassadors to some extent, wanting to do the best parts of our cultures justice. People go out of their way to impress me, and the most gracious response is also the truest one—I am continually impressed.

Sometimes, though, I find myself taking liberties with the eagerness that surrounds me. The telescope, for example, is in many pieces and will take awhile to assemble. Yolanda warns that I shouldn't get my hopes up, that with this bright moon we won't be able to see much. José says that in any case, the moon itself is always interesting. They want to accommodate me, to offer me a more complete experience here. I feel bad asking them to do this, and yet I really want them to. I don't know where this desire comes from, and I don't understand its insistence. But it's clearly connected to the hunger I can't control today.

From early in my time in Spain, I've been aware that emotions can well up in me, sudden and strong. I go about my day, filled almost to bursting with the excitement of living in such a vibrant place, and then suddenly a light goes on and exposes the empty, cobwebbed corners of my mind. After José sets up the telescope and Yolanda determines that Saturn is invisible, I feel those corners intensely. I long to take in, absorb, fill the gaps between my internal and external worlds. At one point I even ask Yolanda for a cigarette, but she knows I don't smoke and refuses to give me one.

We take turns looking at the moon, whose brightness does indeed flood out the rest of the sky, and then Yolanda brings out the marzipan cookies, laughing that her parents aren't going to get a single one. As we indulge yet again, my chest swells with affection, and it's maddening not to have an outlet for it. I need a focal point for this pleasure that threatens to overwhelm my nerves, a canvas onto which I can project and observe it. I want to reach out, drape an arm over a knee, lean my warm body into another. Instead, I take a deep breath and remind myself that this craving, too, will pass. In both English and Spanish, the word *desire* comes from the Latin phrase, *de sidere*, "of the stars." The original meaning may have been "to wait for whatever the stars will bring," a definition I find appealing tonight, in spite of my impatience and with so few stars visible in the sky.

Sleep. After a day spent ingesting, it carries me quickly away, into that realm where the strange and the familiar intermix. Drifting off has never been for me, as it was for Nabokov, a "nightly betrayal of reason, humanity, genius." Rather it's a tremendously pleasurable release from the material world. Sleep is a sinking down into representation, into a glorious land where language is composed of images and sensory impressions and a grammar whose rules remain pleasantly out of reach.

In dreams, nothing shocks. Not hunger, not desire, not the presence of people in places they shouldn't be. Not even José, his long, lean body pressed against mine, here in this small bed that has grown wide enough to accommodate us both. My body feels buoyant, bobbing gently with the gravitational pull and release, the weight of him. And yet I'm down under the surface where waves swell against me, through me, my arms and legs drawing together and apart, propelling me upward toward a diffuse light. The moon shines above in a bright blue sky, and I stretch my legs, my arms, moving faster in order to slow down. "José," I say, and his voice responds from behind my neck, entangled in my hair. "Close your eyes," he tells me gently in Spanish and I do, squeezing tight, trying not to see the surface of the water. Our arms and legs continue to contract until I take a huge breath and hold it, muscles pulsating, then bow my head and break through, released into morning.

I recognize the small room, the clock on the bureau: 7:08 AM. I'm no longer asleep, but I haven't fully come into wakefulness. It was a dream, of course, but there are real physical sensations, real pleasure. My face flushes hot, my eyes open wide. I wonder if I called out in my sleep.

The house is silent. I listen for a moment before getting up and hurrying toward the bathroom. Already I'm rationalizing, even in this barely-awake state: my subconscious has taken my affection for Spain, the constant attractions of my daily life, and given them male form. Of course it would be the form of the man I see most regularly, a man I like very much and appreciate but do not, do not, do not feel attracted to.

As I cross the hallway and reach for the bathroom door, it opens. Before me is the real José, face puffy with sleep, looking—in his boxer shorts and tee shirt—as vulnerable as I feel. We both jump, wide-eyed, then nod hello and scurry around each other. Inside the bathroom I sit down, one hand across my mouth, the other covering my eyes. *Shame on you*, I think, gasping and giggling, feeling more than ever on the verge of losing control.

All day Sunday I'm vigilant. Through breakfast and a hike in the hillside north of town, through a trip to one of the two bars, where we meet up with Yolanda's parents for glasses of sweet vermouth, through the large midday meal followed by the rest of the marzipan cookies, I pretend I don't know the meaning of hunger. I take small portions, refuse seconds, and try not to look at José, at his tall, broad body, olive skin, curly black hair, and his fluid, easy smile.

I have a hard time looking at Yolanda, too. It would be one thing if I'd woken up this morning and laughed off the craziness of the unconscious mind. But this was one of those dreams that lingers, altering the colors and textures of the day, changing the way the breeze feels against my skin. Yesterday was like sleepwalking compared with how sharp my senses are now, how heightened my perceptions. I can't brush away how real the scene felt, the strong pull of its sounds and images, the sexiness of it. Nor do I want to. The dream feels like a shining gold box at my core. I'm aware of it constantly, but only rarely do I peer under its lid and remember the details, my heart racing.

In the afternoon we sit with Yolanda's parents in the backyard. The day has turned balmy beyond belief, as if we've skipped past spring into full-blown summer. We roll our short sleeves up over our shoulders to feel the sun. A family friend stops by, and Yolanda's mother introduces me to her as "the American who doesn't eat meat." I'm slightly embarrassed by the label, but right now I think she could call me far worse things and I'd be hard-pressed to argue.

Just when we're starting to talk about heading back to Oviedo, about how if we leave now we can arrive before dark, the mayor comes through the back gate. I'd met him earlier at the bar, an outgoing and funny man with great pride of place. He says he's been thinking I ought to have a proper tour of the town. Everyone agrees, and we head off as a group, ambling through the streets as the mayor points out landmarks and tells local legends. There are somber stories of drought and concerns for how much longer the town can hold on to its agricultural roots, and there are funny stories about property disputes, including one that led to the cemetery being nicknamed "Gerardo's vegetable garden." We ascend a slight hill and pass through a wrought iron gate into a grassy area with a couple dozen grave markers. The cemetery overlooks the town and the forested hillside beyond, and I squint into the distance, trying to make out where our hike took us this morning. José steps up behind me and leans in, his face hovering just above my shoulder, his cheek nearly touching mine. "There," he says pointing, describing where we picked up the trail and where we came back out again. It's an innocent move, something he could have done yesterday—may well have done yesterday—without my noticing. But today it makes my skin burn.

By the time we get back to the house, the sun is dropping toward the horizon. The mayor says good-bye, and the rest of us sit down again in the lawn chairs, beneath a poplar tree whose buds, we marvel, seem to be growing larger before our eyes. Yolanda and José smoke their last two cigarettes, and I swallow a motion sickness pill in preparation for the drive. Yolanda's mother wants to make us a snack for the trip, but we tell her no. "We've done nothing but eat since we got here!" Yolanda says, and I convincingly agree.

The truth is that I'm less hungry right now than I've been all weekend. Maybe this is connected to our departure, to the fact that in a couple of hours I'll be back home, where I can eat everything in my half of the refrigerator if I want to. Maybe it's because I've made it through this weekend without too many linguistic faux pas and, I believe, without giving Yolanda's family a bad impression of Americans. Maybe it has to do with the relaxation that's overtaking my body here in this lovely yard, or with the mayor's tour, which offered something I didn't know I craved, a sense of living history and community. Or maybe—and this is the explanation I fear—it's because my hunger for food has been translated today into something much more complicated and difficult to appease.

Shortly we'll put our overnight bags into the car and say good-bye to Yolanda's parents. I'll climb into the back seat, from which I'll watch José's shoulders and hair darken as night takes over, transforming him into someone I don't recognize. As the gauzy veil of medication drops behind my eyes, I'll reach into my short-term memory for that golden box and go through the dream, frame by frame. I'll call up the strong emotional and physical sensations of this morning, and after a few moments they'll start to fade. Then I'll step away from memory, listen in on the sounds of Yolanda's voice, José's voice, the radio. I'll let the dream drain away from my conscious mind, and then I'll sidle up to it again, glance over my shoulder, and feel more strongly than ever the purest form of desire.

This weekend is not the first time I've felt like a stranger to myself in Spain. There are constant surprises in my life here, states of having and being and wanting and longing I don't know how to name. Sometimes these states are unpleasant, sometimes they're puzzling, and sometimes they are thrillingly, horrifyingly delicious.

Everyday Lessons

T he post office is busier than usual today. Five lines snake through the cavernous hall, each with its own collection of señoras and señores and *jovenes* like me (because in Spain the term *youth* applies well into one's thirties). We wait patiently, clutching our packages and letters, umbrellas tucked under our arms. It hasn't rained yet this morning, but the sky outside is the color of new cement.

As always, I'm trying to listen in on the conversations around me. I miss the pleasure of eavesdropping, of floating through a web of stories, catching shadowy glimpses of the dramas in other people's lives. It's still difficult for me to understand Spanish out of context, so I practice making sense of the random words my ear picks out. In the next line, a couple talks of visiting someone who is ill, or perhaps being visited by someone who *was* ill, I'm not sure. In front of them two college-aged guys laugh. "No tiene nada que ver," one says, *that's got nothing to do with it,* but I can't get any further with them.

The woman in front of me, her short black ponytail framed symmetrically by bobby pins, glances around and says to no one in particular that it's Wednesday, the middle of the month, why so many people? The man behind me stops whistling and agrees that this wait is very strange, then resumes his warbling tune. I want to respond, to contribute to the social exchange that's always taking place around me. At the bus stop, in the grocery store, wherever we wait together, Spanish people toss comments into the air, invitations to converse that I want to accept. But small talk is almost as difficult for me as eavesdropping. I'm so concerned with speaking correctly, especially to strangers, that I often can't bring myself to voice an observation or annoyance.

Then again, I'm not annoyed by the post office lines, not even curious about why so many people have come here today. I've walked downtown this morning to mail two letters, and there's nothing else on my agenda until I teach at 7:00 tonight. I have all the time in the world. If the weather holds I'll probably sit on a bench in the park and read the newspaper, stop by the public library to look for an easy Spanish novel, then pass through the open-air market on my way home for the midday meal. My life in Spain is like this most of the time, calm and unfettered. Although some days also include private tutoring or freelance translation work, even that doesn't compare to the schedule I kept back in the States. This entire year feels like an extended vacation.

I come from a country, a culture, in which hard work is valued above all else, to a point that's often unhealthy. I know this. And yet I can't escape the twinge of guilt that comes with the relaxed pace of my life here. I spend most of my time reading, studying the language, taking long walks, and accepting weekend invitations to travel. I keep wondering whether I deserve such a privileged existence, whether I've *earned* it. This is the mindset I've brought with me to Spain, a banking system of cosmic balance that I'm trying to shed.

When I first arrived here, excited to teach two eight-month sections of Intermediate English at the University of Oviedo, I was told there'd been a mistake and only one section was available. This was devastating news, since I needed every peseta of my half-time salary to live. I fretted, wrung my hands, asked if something couldn't be done about this problem, because after all I had agreed to teach two courses, not one, I had come all the way to Spain—given up my job and apartment, sold my car—to teach *two* courses. Heads of departments were called, colleagues were consulted, and eventually it was decided that if I were willing, I could teach a section of Beginning English in addition to my Intermediate class. Foreign teachers normally weren't assigned this course because it required giving grammatical explanations in Spanish. Everyone knew I didn't have the language skills for this, but I agreed to do it because I didn't see an alternative. Only after the arrangements had been made did I realize why everyone was so surprised by my insistence: my salary would have been the same either way. Of course they would pay me the agreed-upon amount—but of course! How else would I live? And then I would teach whatever the English department needed me to teach, one course, two courses, but in any case not more than two because that's what my contract said. In the face of this logic, I felt like a perfect American fool.

The line has begun to move, only three more people ahead of me. Silently I practice what I'll say to the clerk: send these first class, give me five post card stamps, and have you gotten more of the air mail stickers you ran out of last week? I'll say all of this in a demanding voice, not in the apologetic tone with which I asked for service in the early months. For a long time I thought it was my accent that made waiters and bartenders walk away before I'd completed an order. I'd be falling all over myself to be polite, trying not to offend anyone, saying "Please, if you don't mind, I'd like . . . ," with a voice so tentative they must have thought I hadn't yet decided. I wasn't paying attention to the abrupt way other people said, "Give me a coffee." "Bring me two beers." Of course they said "thank you" afterward, but there was no polite lead-in to what was truly an *order*. Once I figured this out, it was as if I'd been given a password.

Early on, the effort required for the most minor communication had exhausted me daily. And the amount of time it took to accomplish anything in Oviedo was exasperating. I'd leave my apartment with a list of errands and return home hours later with not one of them crossed off. Offices would have closed early for siesta, or not opened at all because of a regional holiday or a saint's day; administrators would be back in a little while, surely, or tomorrow would be just as good a time, why not come back then? For months I struggled against what seemed to me an impossible way to do business. But gradually my attitude changed, to the point where I no longer think in days. If I make a to-do list now, it's for the entire week, and if, through some miracle, three of the five items are crossed off by Tuesday, I put the list away and take a rest. Weeks pass without my doing what needs to be done, but since deadlines are never very firm in this country, it doesn't matter. Sometimes, I've even discovered, if I wait long enough to make a phone call or file a form with the university, the task becomes unnecessary. Doing too much too quickly has come to seem wrong-headed, even petty, a way of rushing through life and making extra work along the way.

The post office line inches forward, and I'm trying to listen in on a conversation between two men in the next line who seem to be strangers, although one rests a hand on the other's forearm as he speaks. Then a woman passes between us. She's of stout build, somewhere around sixty, wearing a wool skirt, sensible shoes, a sweater that contours her large bosom. She makes her way to the front of my line then stops, facing the clerk as if expecting to be called next. The woman in front of me clears her throat. "Excuse me, señora, the line is here," she says, pointing behind us.

The first woman turns and glances down the length of the line. "I only need stamps," she says, waving her hand in the air.

The whistling behind me stops. "We all need stamps," the man says, "That's why we're waiting." The interloper waves again, fingers brushing alongside her ear. "Just two stamps," she insists.

All at once a chorus erupts: "You have to wait, too." "The back of the line is there." "Come on, señora, don't try to take advantage." The woman protests weakly, then shrugs her shoulders and gives in, making her way to the end of the line.

I'm silent throughout this scene but I very much want to speak, to take my rightful, indignant place in this crowd. I collect my thoughts and decide to say to the man behind me, "¡Qué cosa!"—*what a thing to do!* But when I turn around, I see that his face is relaxed, with no hint of what just happened. The same is true of the woman behind him and the man behind her. Back at the end of the line, the woman who caused the fuss has settled in, wearing a similar expression of patient acceptance. I seem to be the only person aware of what just went on.

In Spain I keep learning the same lessons again and again. Sometimes they're about verb tense or idiomatic expressions, sometimes they're about how to *be* in the world, how to negotiate the dramas of daily life with something like grace. Just last week, I was swimming in the crowded university pool, sharing a lane with a woman who kept bumping me as we passed each other. I had taken my contact lenses out beforehand, so the water was fuzzy beyond my plastic goggles, and I couldn't see her until she was upon me. For ten laps I moved defensively, trying to avoid her slaps and kicks, becoming convinced that she wanted to crowd me out of the lane. Finally, after a full-on collision in the shallow end, I threw my head up and prepared to face her. "Look——" I was about to say, "I was here first, so you must swim over there." I feared she would argue, and I hoped I'd be able to find the words to counter her. Instead, she flipped her goggles up, smiling and squinting, and I could see she was a teenager. "Pardon me," she gasped, "I don't swim well!" My face colored with relief and embarrassment. "Don't worry about it," I told her, and we returned to swimming and bumping.

Always I expect confrontation to be difficult, to turn ugly. Why is that, I wonder, standing in line at the post office and marveling at how easily people here speak their minds. If I'd said "¡Qué cosa!" to the man behind me, my voice would have sounded aggrieved, even vengeful, as if the woman's action had been a personal affront. And if I were the woman who cut in line—not such a stretch, since I often misunderstand signs or protocol—I would be mortified by the others' response. I'd flee the post office immediately, wait until another day to try again. I look back toward the end of the line and feel only admiration for that woman, waiting with such composure to buy her two stamps.

"Grace under pressure" was Hemingway's ideal. It's an attractive mantra even when we're not talking about war and hunting and bullfights. Even when we're talking about everyday scenes of interacting with strangers, of watching and ingesting and waiting to observe one's own response to the unpredictable. Living as a foreigner, negotiating the daily thicket of language, makes grace worth striving for every moment.

Outside the post office, the air is thick and humid and still. Sounds seem intensified—the acceleration of city buses, a man's voice calling across the street, "Oye Martín," the click of heels on the wide post office stairs. I hold the door for the person exiting behind me, a tall, thin elderly woman wearing a tailored lilac suit. She seems well into her seventies, with an erect posture, a gracious way of moving that makes me take note. At the top of the stairs we each pause, checking the sky. "At least the rain hasn't started yet," she says. "No, not yet," I respond, pleased beyond reason with this tiny utterance. Then, as the woman starts down, she catches the heel of one shoe on the second step.

The woman doesn't have time to raise her hands. A young man on the sidewalk below looks up and responds as I do, reaching out across an impossible distance, trying to catch her. There is a moment of flight, a moment when none of her touches the ground, and then her forehead hits the first step below the landing, her lilac suit crumpling with the impact. Others see it, too, from the top of the stairs, from the side, and there's a moment of horrified pause as everyone processes what just happened. Then we all rush to her.

"Cuidado, señora," is all I can manage to say. *Be careful.*

We guide her into a sitting position at the edge of the landing. Someone retrieves her purse while someone else convinces her not to stand. "I'm all right," she says, trying to wave us away, but already her forehead is swelling purple. From the top of the steps a man asks, "Shall I call an ambulance?" and a chorus erupts, "Sí, sí!"

The woman stares ahead, her long fingers trembling. I squat beside her, watching as a mass on her shin engorges and deepens, as her cheeks grow pale and her forehead continues to swell. She sits very still, not speaking, and I do the same because I cannot think of a single comforting thing to say. I wonder what's happening inside her, what damage her body is right now trying to contain. She may have a concussion or broken bones. Or perhaps, miraculously, only bad bruising that will make her sore for a while. I imagine her children hearing of this accident, coming to visit, calling on the phone and warning, too late as I did, "Be careful." Her husband will want to know what happened, how did this fall occur, and she won't be able to explain. But I saw, I know what happened. She caught a heel and tripped, a simple thing that could happen to any of us. And yet at her age, this fall may mark the end of something. The end of freedom, perhaps, of the time when she could count on herself to negotiate the world alone.

Around us, people murmur. How awful, what a shame, *pobrecita.* I'm the only silent one in the crowd. I desperately want to explain that she just caught a heel, but I have no idea how to say this in Spanish. Caught a bus or a fish or a cold, yes, but not the phrase I need right now. My eyes sting and the steps beneath me begin to move. How can I count on myself not to stumble, not to fall hard, when I can't even explain the simple truth of what I see?

An ambulance siren whines in the distance. I look at the translucent skin of her leg, hideously engorged, beneath stockings that didn't even tear. The stairs spin faster, my peripheral vision shimmers white. I rehearse a farewell: "I have to go, I'm sorry, I hope you'll be all right." But then I stand without saying a word and hurry away. This is the opposite of grace under pressure: it's falling apart at the slightest provocation.

I rush down the sidewalk, trying to escape the howl of the siren. I feel like a child on the verge of a tantrum, my surroundings made suddenly strange by the reflex of loss. I crave home, a place of ease and comfort, where women don't fall down stairs and language has the texture of spun silk. Why on earth, I wonder, am I trying to live in Spain?

Instead of going to the park, or the library, or the open-air market, I head for my small, familiar apartment. With each passing block my adrenaline fades, until I understand once again that language isn't really the problem, that life is dangerous everywhere, at all times. I imagine the paramedics checking her blood pressure, stabilizing her neck, easing her onto a stretcher. I imagine going home and asking my housemate how to say "catch a heel," then writing the phrase out and committing it to memory. I will do the only thing I know how to do, as futile as that may be: I'll practice for another day exactly like today.

On Climbing Peña Ubiña

igh in the mountains of southern Asturias, snow gleams with the visual texture of sand. I squint into the glare, pretending the fields we're crossing are the Sahara, the Kalahari, the Gobi, and think of Paul Bowles' *The Sheltering Sky*, how the characters travel deeper and deeper into the desert, not knowing why but unable to turn back. That makes sense to me. This terrain, the steep alpine meadows covered with snow and the jagged peaks into which we're heading, arouses some latent desire to take off into the wilderness, to live in a way that pares everything down to survival. There's a purity above the treeline, a strangeness that both intimidates and consoles.

It's the consolation part I'm after these days. So often we travel for comfort, to get away from something, from everything. That's why I'm living in Spain right now, if I'm to be honest. Two years into an intense romantic relationship, I wanted an emotional rest, a calmer existence for a temporary period of time. And for a while it looked as though everything might work out as I'd hoped, that this separation would enable each of us to get our bearings and continue forward, together. But now heartache has found me here, and the only thing I can think to do in response is travel.

Last week a flyer appeared on the wall outside my office in the English department: "Come on a mountain excursion! Camp in a lodge! Enjoy views of the Spanish Alps! EASY HIKE!" The trip was organized by Enrique, the president of an international social group, who puts together an outing every few weeks for foreigners at the university. I've gone on many of these trips but avoided the hikes because people always return from them limping and cursing. So I didn't believe the poster's promise, but I was drawn to a change in surroundings and even, perversely, to the physical pain I might suffer afterward.

Now, two hours into the journey, I'm already suffering. No one expected this much snow in May, not even Enrique. We're in up to our knees, thirty people goose-stepping along in a line, each of us using the same set of footprints. My hiking boots have soaked through. My thighs burn, my lower back throbs, the wind makes my shoulders hunch up around my ears. When the line stops moving, I lean to the side and see dozens of jackets rippling like colorful sails above a pure white sea. The sky is pale blue with clouds so thin they barely cast a shadow before disappearing into the valley behind us. I take a long, deep breath, trying to inhale something essential, something that has to do with perspective and context. The fields are unending, the glacier-carved peaks ahead seem no closer than they were an hour ago. But I'm not complaining, not even to myself. I'm just taking things in.

Enrique jogs back and forth, agile as a leopard, calling for a five-minute rest. He's full of energy and charm, which is why people keep coming on these trips. The backpack he carried up to the lodge yesterday contained six liters of milk and half a kilo of dark chocolate, and the first thing he did upon arriving was make a vat of hot cocoa that transported us all back to childhood. Today he's dressed entirely in red—boots, snowsuit, a bandana tied around his jet black hair. Anyone else would look silly. In his right hand he carries a pickaxe, but I don't have the courage to ask him what it's for.

There's nowhere to sit or lean, so we stand in our tracks, twisting our upper bodies around to talk to one another. Most of us are students or teachers from abroad, a few are Spaniards. Enrique's brought some buddies who, like him, have been climbing these mountains almost since they could walk, and I've brought Lola and José, both experienced hikers. José's partner, Yolanda, is away in England right now for a six-week language course, and it's her absence that enabled me to come on this trip: I saw the poster but didn't have hiking gear, so José rifled through Yolanda's closet and found me some boots, a sleeping bag, and a headband to keep my ears warm. Lola contributed a backpack and, as so often happens in my daily life in Spain, in the space of a few hours I found myself ready for something I hadn't expected.

Lola says her hair is driving her crazy, blowing into her eyes, so we make a trade: my headband for her sunglasses. José stands behind me, looking handsome with his coat zipped up to his chin. Together we scan the peaks ahead, their gaps and crevices coated with ice, then ask Enrique which one is Peña Ubiña. "You can't see it from here," he says nonchalantly. "It's behind that far ridge." José's eyebrows rise up above his sunglasses at that one.

As usual, José wears a somber expression that breaks easily into a smile. He's tall with short, dark hair, high cheekbones, an olive skin tone that contrasts with many people here in the North. He reminds me of the rich Moorish influence in Spain, the art, architecture, language, genes. Everything about him appeals to me. I became aware of this several weeks ago, after an amorous dream about José that occurred while I was spending the weekend with him and Yolanda in the country. Upon waking in the early morning, I got up and headed to the bathroom, nearly running into José in the hall. For the rest of the day—and for quite a while after that—I felt under the spell that coincidence often casts, convinced on an irrational level that something had passed between us.

Enrique announces that the snow is really slowing us down, we'll have to hurry. The marching begins again, and my body's motion frees my mind to float through the recent, thorny past. That first startling dream about José was just the beginning. Every night afterward my subconscious played out storylines that made me feel excited and guilty in the morning. Soon the dreams developed into daytime fantasies, and I began to feel as though I were having an affair. Each time I saw Yolanda or José felt like an out-of-body experience, the imaginative part of me watching the saner part converse as if nothing were amiss. It was maddening and delightful at once—and addictive, as desire often is.

I started to think about the ethics of an affair. Once Yolanda left for England, it would be the perfect set-up, a defined period that no one would ever have to know about. If we were obsessively discrete, I reasoned, if neither Yolanda nor my boyfriend in New York ever found out, would it really be such a hurtful thing to do?

The main obstacles were two. Yolanda, because I couldn't imagine betraying a female friend that way; and José, because I had no reason to think he was interested in an affair. Nonetheless, the moral principles fascinated me, and as a way of wrestling with them I started writing a short story that dealt with exactly this situation. A man, a woman, an opportunity. The question at the heart of the story was: Is there a way to betray humanely, to act badly with some degree of grace? The answer I was writing toward was, of course, yes.

All of this took place just before my own trip back to upstate New York for the Easter break. I'd wanted to spend that time traveling in Spain, taking a last, leisurely look at the country I've fallen in love with. But the man in New York had visited me in January, and he begged me to return the favor in April. He missed me terribly, he said, arguing that sometimes you have to make concessions for the long-term good of a relationship. Finally, reluctantly, I agreed.

On the flight to New York, I worked on my story, still delighting in the impulse toward an affair. Midway across the Atlantic I realized how little like fiction the story would seem if the man in New York were to read it, and I spent the last part of the flight translating what I'd written into Spanish. I threw the English pages out before we landed, feeling almost as excited by the presence of my Spanish-speaking self on the page as by the plot I was working out. I looked forward to finishing the story during the vacation, then translating it back into English on my way home to Spain.

Then, two days later, irony burst onto the scene. We were out running errands, driving along North Chestnut Street in New Paltz, when he said he had something to tell me. At first it seemed he was relating a story, so casual and calm was his voice, and then he began to get nervous, stopping and starting and taking deep breaths in the rhythm of confession. He talked through the red light and onto Main Street, up the hill toward the grocery store, but instead of turning into the parking lot, he just kept driving and talking.

Later the drama would begin, the anger and tears, the accusations. But during that car ride I could think only of the magic of coincidence, the collusion of inevitability and surprise. I was stunned silent as he talked, less by the affair he described than by the sense that I had somehow authored it.

Finally, we exhaust the open space we've been crossing for hours and find ourselves at the base of a very steep hill. When I look back in the direction we came from, I'm surprised to see that the valley has been replaced by yet another ridge. All this time I thought we were walking due south, but in fact we've curved around to the back side of some peaks. Enrique points uphill to our right, where there's an area of boulders and brown grass, and says we'll take our next break there. It doesn't look very far away, but lately I don't trust my judgment.

I follow Lola's lead, serpentining back and forth up the hill and stopping periodically to admire the view, which is a ruse to keep from throwing up. I'm in pretty good shape these days, I swim three times a week and my primary mode of transportation is walking, but this is no "easy" hike. Nor was the "lodge" where we spent last night a lodge. It was an A-frame cabin with no heat, no plumbing, and a dozen cots for thirty hikers. After a night of lying on the floor unable to sleep, I began today wondering if this trip was a mistake. The magic of travel doesn't work so well when what you're trying to get away from is your own mind. Six thousand feet up in the Cordillera Cantábrica mountain range, I'm filled with the same dilemmas I've come here to escape.

In my Intermediate English class, I've been teaching students about conditional verbs—what could happen, should have been, might be *if*. They're having a hard time, and I've been tempted more than once to tell them not to bother, that the conditional is overrated anyhow. Let's just stick to the facts, I want to say, and make all of our lives easier.

The "ifs" are driving me crazy. When I returned from New York the week before last, I had the worst insomnia of my life. Each night I worked myself into a frenzy by thinking through the different scenarios, until it was 4:00 AM and I was sitting on the couch watching American westerns dubbed in Spanish. So I made a deal with myself: think about "the New York problem" all day if you have to. Write letters that you will or won't send, imagine elaborate scenarios of reconciliation. But once the pajamas are on and the lights go out, push him out of your mind. Erect barriers that memory cannot scale.

I needed a lot of those barriers last night, lying at the end of a row of sleeping bags, listening to the steady breathing of everyone around me and feeling, in a room with thirty people, as lonely as I've ever been. I tried to distract myself, thinking about how much snow there is at this elevation and about the lack of a bathroom, which is a bigger problem for the women than for the men, and about Lola, who seems to be having a good time, and José, who seems quieter than usual. I thought about the ache in my lower back, wondering whether it was from carrying a heavy backpack or from the beginnings of menstrual cramps, and then I thought about what I'll do if my period doesn't come this week or next. That would be the icing on my stale cake, I thought, rolling my eyes in the dark. Then I took a deep breath, led my mind away from the precipice, and began to count *ovejas* in Spanish. I got to 700 before the sun began to rise.

Now, by the light of day, no thoughts are forbidden.

How different things would be if I'd had an affair with José. How different things would be if I'd had an affair with anyone. If my response to all his talking had been, "How about that! Me, too!"

Do I still think it's possible to betray with decency, to act badly with some degree of grace? I stubbornly think I do. If I'd had an affair, I would have done it differently. Not blatantly, not so that he'd ever walk into a room and have other people search his face to see whether he knew. Of that much I'm sure.

A spot of sadness throbs like a bruise along my breastbone. A month from now I'll be back in upstate New York, with no car and no job and nowhere to live. I'd been planning to move in with him, into a lovely old farmhouse at the base of a mountain. He'd said I could share his car until I got one of my own, and he'd written letters about what a great reunion we would have, filled with long days of peaceful adjustment. Now he doesn't understand why I'm rethinking those plans, why something as simple and common as an affair has to get in the way.

A small, hard stone of anger rattles around in my stomach. I think, for perhaps the ninetieth time, that I agree with him in principle. That it's not the affair that infuriates me but the cowardice, the gall of bringing me back from Spain in order to clear his conscience. Why not just tell me over the phone, I'd asked, and he'd said he feared I might never come back to him. Why not just wait until I returned in June? Because he didn't want someone else to tell me first. A balloon of anger swells inside my throat until I have to pause again, turn around, pretend to admire the view. The truth is I don't want to climb Peña Ubiña. But I do want, desperately, to reclaim my delight at living in Spain.

"We're almost there!" Enrique shouts. Back and forth we huff, groaning. At least the snow has thinned out so we no longer have to lift our knees high with every step. We climb for ten more minutes, then ten more, then five, until we reach the lip of the hill and, one by one, fall down panting. My various throbbing body parts merge into one holistic ache.

In the last week I've fantasized constantly about physical injury — falling down a flight of stairs, breaking an arm or an ankle. I'd like to wear a cast right now, to carry a visible sign that something's wrong. Then people would ask what happened and I would tell the story, point to the wound, have everything out in the open. That would be better, I think, than continuing the way I am now: healthy in appearance, but feeling as if my internal organs might burst through my skin.

Lola hands me half a chocolate bar. Around us, people lounge on the rocks, examining blisters, changing into dry socks. I lean back and close my eyes, letting the warm sun counter the wind and listening to the intermittent languages of the people around me. Dutch, Arabic, Spanish, German — there are so many languages in the world, I think, in which to tell our stories. So many stories, and so many of them sad.

Seated a little ways from me is an Italian man who, until recently, was dating my friend Sophie from France. I think about how much worse Sophie's Easter break was than mine, how fortunate I am by comparison. She and the Italian spent a week traveling around Spain with some friends, and according to the friends, the Italian wanted to break up with Sophie but couldn't muster the nerve. His behavior was erratic: one day he'd be buying her gifts, the next he'd be meaner than a snake or he'd disappear in the middle of the afternoon and not come back until the next day. Sophie couldn't relax for worry and confusion. She hardly slept, drank and smoked too much, ate very little. When they got back to Oviedo, she collapsed and spent the next ten days unconscious. It wasn't a coma, the intensive care doctors insisted, but whatever virus she'd contracted was attacking her internal organs. They put her on a respirator and then, when her kidneys started to fail, on a dialysis machine. Her parents came from France, a priest performed last rites, and every time the phone rang I jumped out of my skin.

Then, as inexplicably as Sophie fell ill, she began to improve. When we left Oviedo yesterday, she was awake and able to blink her eyes in response to questions, but she still can't breathe on her own. The Italian, meanwhile, is climbing Peña Ubiña. As raw as I feel right now, I don't have it in me to form an opinion about that.

One by one we stand up, rewrapping our chocolate and cookies, trying to summon enough energy for the next leg of the climb. "The summit is just over there," Enrique says for the tenth time. All I can see is a rock wall, but I have something like faith in this nutty guy dressed all in red, this man who derives so much pleasure from gathering us together, feeding us hot cocoa, leading us farther than anyone cares to go.

Enrique waves his axe like a baton and shouts, "¡Vámonos!" He smiles and winks, and like a herd of enthusiastic sheep, we follow him. We scramble over loose rocks and giant boulders, using our arms as well as our legs to climb. We slip and bang our shins, and when my foot gets caught in a crevice, I yank it out and tear a gash clear through the side of Yolanda's boot. José assures me it's no big deal and insists I take off the boot and show him that my foot is unharmed. Three weeks ago this tenderness would have undone me, and even now, when he squats down and examines my wet sock, a look of concern on his face, the breath catches in my throat.

This part of the climb is more dangerous, but I'm glad for the chance to use new muscles. We ascend rapidly now, making measurable progress, although each time we scale a section and stand up to get our bearings, we discover yet another wall ahead. People start to complain, but Enrique waves away their concern, then rushes off to scout the conditions. He's determined to eat lunch at the summit.

Soon we're shuffling along an icy ledge beside a sheer, fifty-meter drop. I'm so focused on finding a piece of rock to hold onto as I move around a curve into the wind that the level of danger doesn't sink in. Then someone in the back shouts, "¡Basta, Enrique!" *Enough!* This is really dangerous, people say, we need ropes for climbing on this kind of ice. I hold my breath as Enrique returns, dancing past me on the ledge and arguing that we'll be fine as long as we're careful. I can't see what's going on behind me, and when I finally navigate my way onto a large, flat rock, our ranks have dwindled to fifteen.

"They turned back because they're afraid," Enrique says with a frown, pushing at the air with his hand. "And what a shame because we're almost there."

I begin to feel superstitious. I think of Sophie lying in the hospital right now, a machine pumping air into her lungs, and I wonder why we're tempting fate this way. The world is such a dangerous place, shouldn't we try to protect ourselves in any way we can? I admire the folks who gave up, who are right now heading down out of this wind, enjoying the spectacular views we continue to keep at our backs.

Not far from the summit, I finally lose my nerve. A narrow ravine stands between us and a snowy rock barely wide enough for two people to stand on. After jumping we'll have to scale a wall of snow, into which Enrique has carved holes for hands and feet with his axe. I look over the edge of the ravine and see a tremendous depth ending in bare rock. My stomach cramps tightly. "I should have turned back," I say to Lola and José, who are both behind me, and then I look to the woman in front of me, the next one to cross the ravine. She's a muscular, outdoorsy Belgian, and I expect her to scoff and say there's nothing to this. Instead she says, "This is ridiculous, someone's going to get killed."

"That's it, I'm done," I announce, but Lola blocks my way. She's petite, with chocolate eyes and a smile that comes easily to her always red lips, but right now her expression is fierce. She leans around me and commands the Belgian to jump, and she does. I follow, but only after realizing that if I fell, crashing to my death on the rocks below, the man in New York would spend the rest of his life feeling guilty. He would understand that if I hadn't been in this distraught frame of mind, if I didn't have something to prove—to him and to myself—I would never have been so foolish.

At the summit, Enrique keeps shouting, "*This* is Peña Ubiña!" It is spectacular. Awesome. Humbling. Mountain range after mountain range echoes into the distance, the land rippling away in clouds of rock and snow. The color scheme is pale blue, gray, and white, and the most beautiful spaces of all are the shadows, the places where sunlight falls and then, abruptly, does not. It's an entirely different world up here, a perspective we couldn't have gotten any other way. Even in an airplane, I think, we'd miss the view from eye-level, the straight-on distance and majesty of what feels like the top of the world.

Someone jokes that they can see all the way to France, and again I think of Sophie, of how sad it is that she can't be here with us. Things can always be so much worse than they are, I think, and I join the others in triumphal shouting, our voices carried away by the strong wind. We began this hike at 8:00 in the morning, and it's now 1:30 in the afternoon. How very satisfying to have arrived here, so far above where we started out, purely through the strength of our own bodies.

For several minutes I stand transfixed, expecting that this air, this vista, will cleanse me. But although the sun is warm on my face, the wind begins to penetrate my jacket, my scarf, my sweater, my tee shirt. It burrows through my skin into the organs below. Lola's teeth begin to chatter, and José squats against a stone monument, trying to dodge the gusts. Even Enrique in his red snowsuit starts to shiver. There's talk of leaving immediately, but then someone mentions how hard that last part was and how shaky our muscles feel. So we break out the lunch bags and eat more quickly than is comfortable. In twenty minutes, we're heading back down.

Lola laments not being able to enjoy the summit, but I don't care at all about that. I'm elated, not only because we climbed Peña Ubiña but because we've earned the relief of descending. The hard stuff is behind us, I think giddily, and my chest swells, emotions careening the way they always do during a period of sorrow.

Soon we've negotiated the tricky parts, the snowy wall and the icy ledge, then scrambled down the rocks to the lip of the steepest hill. The cliffs cast long shadows across the meadows below us, and in their darkness, we can see the thin, ghostly line of disturbed snow where we trudged earlier. The line seems to go on forever, and we gather at the edge of the hill to consider our dilemma. It's after 3:00 PM now. It took more than five hours to reach the summit. Even if it takes only half that time to reach the lodge, we still have to pack our things and walk an hour back to the bus, which is supposed to pick us up at 6:00 PM. We aren't going to make it no matter what, but if we could just shave an hour off our time, the bus might still be waiting. We stand in a clump, looking at the hill below. Too bad we don't have sleds, someone says, and then someone else says, don't we? Won't our jackets slide?

A German woman offers to give it a try. We watch in excitement as she pulls her collar up around her ears, tucks the bottom of her jacket around her hips, flops down on her back, feet and head in the air. Enrique gives her a gentle nudge and away she goes. We shout with delight, then gasp as she reaches the bottom of the hill, which levels out toward some rocks. Without even trying, she slows down midway to the rocks and jumps up, arms waving above her head. We clap and shriek like children. Two by two, people line up and take off until everyone has gone except José and me. "This will be great," we tell each other, waiting until the people below us are clear of our path. I'm trying to summon my courage, to lie down and let gravity take me where it wishes. I want to prove to myself that I'm as brave as I'd like to be, as fearless and secure as I was just three weeks ago. And José may be trying to do the same, to let go of what he suspects and I'll soon learn: that Yolanda's trip to England is the beginning of the end for them. Like me, José may be taking deep breaths and trying to keep the panic at bay, reconciling himself to a future in which he might have only himself to rely on.

We lie down at the same time and shove off. It's a great ride, although my cloth jacket slows me some, and when I finally reach the bottom, my clothes—right down to the underwear—are soaked through. But I feel exhilarated. We all do. We're wet but not too cold, and we start talking about the bottles of bourbon back at the lodge and the *sidra*, waiting at the bar in the town below. We hurry through the long, sloping meadows, egging each other on until someone suggests that we try running downhill, leaning back to maintain our center of gravity. What's the worst that can happen? someone shouts, and now it's Enrique who cautions us to slow down and be careful.

We keep to the center of the fields to avoid twisting our ankles on underlying rocks and use gravity to the fullest. Leaning back for balance, we take long jumping strides, each foot sliding a meter when it hits the snow. We leap, land with a whoosh, leap again, until we're literally running down a mountainside. Even the occasional tumbles, which everyone takes, don't dampen our spirits. We sing and giggle, shaking our hips as we dance toward the lodge we can now see below. My body is completely exhausted, my mind liberated. All I think about is the next step, the next feeling of weightless abandon.

Our arrival at the lodge involves high-fiving each other and harassing the group of quitters we find standing around in the sun. Lola heads up to the third floor to change her clothes and José goes in search of our backpacks. Meanwhile, I sip from the bottle of bourbon that's being passed around and think about the crush I had on José so recently. How thrilling it was to inhabit that fantasy, to move through the days with an alternate reality inside me! I can't imagine a real affair being as marvelous as that was, and I'm angry all over again because the real affair in New York has taken even the pleasure of that desire away from me.

Inside the lodge, I ascend to the third floor, which smells of wood shavings and mildew. Hunching below the slanted ceiling, I lay out clean clothes and a towel, then take off my coat, sweater, tee shirt, and bra. The relief of damp skin exposed to air brings tears to my eyes, and I struggle again with the sadness, the fury. I dry my upper half and dress it, then peel off my pants and underwear, which are saturated not only with melted snow but with a wash of watercolor blood. "Oh no!" I cry out, startling a Spanish woman changing nearby. I wrap a towel around my waist and fish through my bag for a tampon, then stand up again and burst out laughing. The pendulum has swung back for a moment, the skies have brightened, my heart soars. My own body, at least, has not betrayed me, and I'm thankful beyond measure for this day, this trip, this snowy mountainside in northern Spain, where everything suddenly seems exactly as it should be.

Body Language

Virginia Woolf once referred to the day she had her long hair cut short like a man's as the most liberating day of her life. I was thinking about that as I entered an airy, second-floor salon in downtown Oviedo one afternoon. I'd been to this salon half a dozen times before, and on each occasion a stylist named Clari, a woman with defiantly short hair and large black eyes, had run her fingers along my scalp and said, "Just a trim? Really?" From the first time we'd met, Clari had been eager to cut my hair, which was thick and straight and fell to the middle of my back.

On this June afternoon—for in Spain 6:00 PM is still afternoon—I sat down in Clari's chair and tried to say the words nonchalantly. "Cut it all off." I was thinking of Virginia Woolf, of lightness and freedom, and I was especially thinking that my time in Spain was coming to an end, and I wanted a visible way to mark the change in my internal landscape. "As short as yours," I told Clari, and her eyes widened with concern. I pointed to her head and said it again. "Like yours. Really. I'm tired of hair." Then I settled in, feeling courageous and proud. Which is how Virginia Woolf must have felt the day she was transformed, how Gertrude Stein, too, may have felt when Alice B. Toklas turned her bun into a butch cut. Stein was delighted with the result, which she thought made her look like a monk, even though her good friend Picasso recoiled. It's easy to imagine Picasso's look of disapproval, the pressed lips trying to be polite. Think of all those portraits, all the beautiful, seductive women he loved and loved and loved. Nearly all of them with long hair.

I enjoyed coming to this salon, with its wooden floors, high ceilings, and long French doors that overlooked a busy street. On this day the doors stood open, inviting a soft summer breeze to swirl around us, and the rhythmic music made me feel hipper than I'd ever been. But what I loved most about coming here was observing Clari. She was a striking woman, with black hair so short it outlined her face, following the upper edge of her forehead, the contour of her temple. She had flawless, light coffee skin, a wide mouth with perfect teeth, tiny unpierced ears. Her eyebrows were thick and perfectly arched, her dark eyes unflinching. She was petite, with strong arms and hands, her thin body dressed always in white—white pants, white tee shirt, a thick black belt between them. Clari had style, a quality that was more than the sum of her parts. In her presence I felt both intimidated and emboldened.

Much of my time in Spain was spent observing women. Often I felt like an adolescent, casting about for older girls to model myself after, except that they weren't always older. Many of the women I observed were students in the university English classes I taught. I studied their clothes and hairstyles and manner of moving as if it were another language, the physical counterpart of the Spanish I was trying to master. Even girls on the street impressed me, teens wearing boiled wool jackets and skirts that fell above the knee, with matching tights and trendy workboots in rose and sky blue. They walked along in pairs, arms linked, their rapid-fire words swirling around me. I envied these girls for what seemed to be a comfort in their public bodies. If they felt awkward or self-conscious, they masked it not with the defensive behaviors of my own adolescence—laughing in shrieks, hiding behind long strands of hair—but by anchoring themselves in the quiet gestures of friendship. Their body language was infused with *cariño*, a word that means something like warmth, affection, good will that's tied less to mood than to a way of being in the world.

Boys and men, too, impressed me with their physicality. Male friends, whether adolescents or adults, touched each other constantly as they walked down the street. One draped an arm over another's shoulder—not with the momentary, joking affection of American men but in a sustained way. Or they walked close together, shoulders touching, heads bowed intimately as they spoke, and when they stopped to greet an acquaintance, one man's hand went around to the small of the other's back, resting there as they chatted. Later, back in the United States, I would fall in love with a man who, perhaps because he had lived in Portugal for a time, touched other men this way.

For now, though, during this year of watching, I longed to absorb some of the bodily comfort I witnessed in the people around me.

Clari stopped snipping for a moment and rustled my suddenly short hair to shake out the loose pieces. "Chica," she said, "you're going to look beautiful. But I want to leave some bangs for now. We can take them away later if you want." She gently positioned my head at a tilt and went to work again.

Once, a couple of years before, I'd asked a graduate school friend to recommend a good salon because I was thinking of having my hair cut short. Before she could respond, a male classmate intervened. "Don't do it!" he exclaimed as if I were leaning out a tenth-story window, "I *love* your hair." He told me how beautiful long hair looks and feels on a woman, how sexy, and although he wasn't someone whose opinion about most things mattered to me, his enthusiasm was infectious. Since then I'd thought of his words with surprising frequency as I continued to negotiate long hair—pulling it back or up, untangling and conditioning it. My hair was more trouble than it was worth, I often thought, but the image of femininity my former classmate had extolled somehow kept me from making a change. Now, watching Clari in the mirror as bits of hair fell onto my shoulders, into my lap, I wondered why I'd let a man I barely knew influence me for such a long time. And why had I resisted the influence of Clari, who was so much more impressive, so much more seductive?

Clari worked meticulously. She narrowed her eyes, staring at something on my head that I couldn't see, then snipped here, combed there, snipped again. Every now and then she'd catch me looking at her in the mirror and smile slightly, her concentration broken. Finally she put down the scissors and picked up an electric razor, asking me to bow my head. With short, gentle strokes she shaved my neck, then leaned in and blew hard to scatter the hairs. My arms tingled, my face flushed. Again I heard the buzz of the razor, again the short strokes, the breath. When I raised my head and looked in the mirror, I did appear—for a brief moment—beautiful. My face seemed thinner, more angular, my eyes larger. Already I had trouble remembering what I'd looked like before.

In the mirror I could see the clock on the wall: 6:40 PM. At 7:00 PM I had to give a final exam to my Intermediate English students, and since classes in Spain always start ten or fifteen minutes late, there was plenty of time. I took a deep breath and imagined walking into the classroom, the way everyone would gasp and exclaim at my new hairstyle. I was fond of this group of students and looked forward to surprising them on our last evening together.

Clari paused, smiling with approval, one hand resting on her hip. I smiled back.

"What made you decide to change your look?" she asked.

I shrugged, suddenly shy, and said I'd wanted something different, something cooler for summer.

She watched me steadily in the mirror. "Have you had trouble with a man?" I stared back, trying to remember whether I'd told Clari about the man in New York, the one who, until recently, I'd planned to move in with when I returned from Spain.

"Women often cut their hair after a break-up," Clari explained, winking and pointing to her own head. Then she leaned close to me, her chin almost resting on my shoulder, her breath warm on my ear. "If you really want a change, an absolutely gorgeous change, you should try a new color." She smiled, her eyebrows arcing perfectly.

How I'd miss her, I thought. How I'd miss the adventures of every-day life—the haircuts, the trips to the grocery store, answering the telephone and hoping I'd be able to understand. How I'd miss the constant pressure of thinking hard about language and meaning, nego-tiating more successfully at some times than others the gaps between them. I told Clari I'd been wanting to change my hair color, perhaps to auburn, although I hadn't really considered it before.

"Perfect," she said. "Let's make an appointment for next week."

I'd imagined saying farewell to Clari as I left the salon, informing her in a casual way that I wouldn't be back. It was too hard other-wise, this closing down of a life, with so many good-byes. But now I blurted out as if confessing, "I can't! Next week I'm moving back to the United States."

Clari inhaled quickly through her teeth. "Next week? Do you really mean *next* week?"

"On Monday," I said, and we stared at each other's reflections for a moment, absorbing the news. We weren't friends. She was a hairstylist and I was her client. Our conversations hadn't been extensive or very personal over the past months, but they'd been a source of curiosity for each of us. Clari was intrigued by my Americanness, by my having moved to Oviedo alone to teach English at the university. And I was intrigued by the kind of life she led. She'd told me once that she lived with some friends on the plaza near city hall. It was a slightly run-down area of nineteenth-century stone buildings, their long windows hung with geraniums and ivy. I imagined Clari's apartment to be bright and airy like the salon but with an ancient scent to it, the walls oozing history. Late at night, there would be a crowd of stylish intellectuals, young men and women gathered to drink wine and espresso and talk about politics, people as engaged and as centered as Clari seemed to be—this woman with short, short hair and a strong personality and the kind of confidence I'd come to Spain hoping to cultivate.

We studied each other for a few moments in the mirror, and it felt to me that we were adjusting to loss, to a thin connection about to be severed. Then Clari held up one finger. She disappeared into the back room where I could hear women talking. Tomorrow was Friday, the salon's busiest day of the week, and I hoped she was trying to squeeze me into her schedule. But when she returned, she said, "*Mira*, I've arranged for another stylist to take my next client. I'll dye your hair right now."

It was a lovely gesture, a parting gift. My face colored as I said thank you, thank you so much, but I couldn't possibly. I have to give a final exam . . . the last class of the year . . . my students . . . but already she was laying out color charts and asking me to choose. When I continued to protest, Clari waved her hand in the air above my head. "Your students?" she said, laughing. "¡Chica! Your students will wait. For this look, they will be happy to wait all night."

Think of Medusa. Lady Godiva. Delilah, who understood so well the power of hair. Think of Mia Farrow's $5,000 cut on the set of *Rosemary's Baby*, photographed as a publicity event. There's a potency not just to hair but to the change in hair, the transformation of locks into snakes, the blurring of feminine and masculine, the cuts and colors and styles that tell us something about who we are. Or were. Or want to be.

I wasn't thinking of any of this as the summer breeze swirled around me, but the legacy of women's hair affected me on an unconscious level. It made me defiant, lured me to the edge of irresponsibility, kept me in the chair for much longer than I should have allowed. When

Clari finally said, "There!" and I stood up, feeling giddy and exposed and utterly transformed, it was after 7:30 PM. Even by Spanish standards, I was very late for my class.

I said thank you and thrust money into Clari's hand, wanting to get out the door quickly. But the other stylists came over to examine my new look, turning me around, cooing and smiling and touching my head. "Oh, you'll be gorgeous in New York," they said, then kissed me on both cheeks, saying good-bye, good luck, have a happy life. Come back someday to Oviedo, they said, and I promised I would.

At the door Clari kissed me, too, and squeezed my hand. "¡Adios! ¡Buena suerte!" she called as I ran down the steps to the street. I kept running, along Calle Uría, through San Francisco Park, up the wide staircase in front of the Guardia Civil headquarters, feeling the change. My hair no longer brushed against my shoulders. And already Clari was someone who used to cut it, someone I'd once known and admired a great deal.

In the College of Sciences, I took the stairs two at a time, panting and sweating. The building was deathly quiet because final exams were in session, except for mine. I pulled the classroom door key from my bag as I ran down the corridor to where my students sat in clumps on the floor. While they jumped to their feet, I gasped and panted apologies. One young man, Javier, had asked me ahead of time how long the test would last and whether he'd be able to make an 8:30 PM ballet performance downtown. When I'd told him absolutely, he'd bought a ticket, even invited me to go along. Now he'd never make it.

"I'm sorry, I'm sorry," I said, bending over to catch my breath. I'd come up with several excuses on the way, but instead of offering one I simply confessed. "I was at the *peluquería* and decided at the last minute to change the color. Javier? Where is he? I'm so sorry. Go—go to the ballet, and I'll meet you tomorrow to give you the exam."

But no one was listening. "It's magnificent!" they beamed, taking hold of my arms and turning me around. "Oh yes, very magnificent!" Even Javier smiled with delight and said, "You look completely Spanish," which was the consensus from everyone. The new hair, the cut and style and especially the color, which was not auburn so much as a kind of burnt orange, was very Spanish.

Throughout the exam, as I tried to calm down and keep my hands away from my forehead, my neck, my ears tickled by the air, students—especially the women I'd been watching so closely all term—would look up from their papers, catch my eye, and smile in approval. The most liberating day of her life, Virginia Woolf had said, and why was that? She'd done something unexpected, erased a part of herself that had held her in a kind of tyranny. Suddenly she was able to communicate without saying a word. I am this. I am not that. And the proof is here on my head, in what I've had the courage to cast off.

At 8:45 PM, Javier turned in his paper. I apologized again, but he shook his head, smiling. "There's no problem," he said without hurry. "I'm going there now. I won't have missed much."

I couldn't look him in the eye when we wished each other well. As Joyce Carol Oates once remarked, "It's the kindnesses we haven't earned and don't deserve that break our hearts." My students, especially Javier, had a right to be angry, but no one was. They'd been concerned about me was all, and when I showed up with what looked like an entirely new head, they had forgiven my self-indulgence and understood what it meant. That I didn't want to leave them. That I wanted now what I'd wanted all along, to emulate their strength and style and cariño, to translate my experience in their country into a language I might one day speak without trying.

Part Two. Madrid, Altamira, Guernica

On Dining Alone

hen I began to travel in a serious way, in a way that went beyond study abroad and short vacations, I was in my early twenties, a year out of college and working two part-time jobs. I'd managed to save a little money but had no other resources for changing my unhappy situation, until on a late spring afternoon, with a breeze blowing promise through the open window, I thought of going away. Perhaps I needed a break from routine, a way to unmoor myself and change the way I thought about the future. A month seemed like a good amount of time, a month-long trip to . . . I thought for a while about all the places I'd never been, which was most of the places there are, and settled on the Swiss Alps. The Alps seemed right because at that stage of my life I felt small, insignificant, and I thought that walking through an external landscape that reinforced this perspective might help me feel more at peace. Which, as it turned out, is exactly what happened.

I understood that I would have to go alone, since none of my friends had the plane fare or vacation days to come along. I wasn't someone who enjoyed time alone, but the decision to untether myself from familiarity, from the comfort of relying on others while moving about in the world, was exhilarating. Addicting. As was the eventual pleasure of accompanying myself almost anywhere I wanted to go.

When I began to travel alone, I had a strict budget and low expectations, especially when it came to meals. Good food was cheap food, eaten on a bench or standing against a crowded counter, on the way to somewhere else. I enjoyed sampling foreign cuisines, but my greatest pleasure came from other senses, from the sights and sounds of a place, the feel of it on my skin. Perhaps I avoided sit-down restaurants, even inexpensive ones, because as a single woman I felt more comfortable moving than lingering. Or maybe at that age and with so little travel experience under my belt, I didn't yet feel entitled to my place at the public table. Now I do. I feel worthy of good food and good wine, and I'm willing to economize on where I sleep in order to spend more of my travel budget in restaurants. And yet dining alone, even now that I've come to enjoy solitude, to prefer sometimes my own company to anyone else's, is never an easy task.

Books, journals, newspapers, postcards—like many solo travelers I use all these props to negotiate meals in public places. At home, where I often eat alone, I enjoy concentrating on the food, staring into the middle distance while my mind drifts through Proustian exhibits of memory. But when I'm in a restaurant, away from familiar territory and feeling slightly apprehensive, slightly guarded, the pleasures of ingestion become more complex. As I wait for and then consume my meal, I know that I, too, am being consumed, a single woman on display, a woman toward whom some people sneak glances while others stare outright. *What is her story?* I can feel them thinking. *What leads her to this restaurant—all alone—on a Friday night in Madrid?*

In my late twenties, I spent a marvelous year living in northern Spain, teaching at a university and immersing myself as fully as possible in a new language and culture. Now, years later, I've come back to this country for research at Madrid's Prado Museum and, perhaps more importantly, to reconnect with the part of myself that lived so well here. I've missed Spanish cuisine, the fresh seafood and rich sauces, and the rhythms of the day's repasts: a small breakfast mid-morning, the largest meal around 3:00 in the afternoon, a light supper at 10 or 11:00 PM, with plenty of snacks in between. While living in Spain I seemed to eat constantly, and yet I lost fifteen pounds in just a few months, the extra weight evaporating into my daily routine.

In Madrid, I feel keenly the complicated pros and cons of traveling alone. Each morning the desk clerk at my hotel offers a voucher for breakfast at a nearby bistro, where I happily order toast and café con leche. Breakfast is never difficult, perhaps because it comes so early in the day and has so much ahead of it. It's a functional meal, aimed at energizing, getting us going, and I feel comfortable in my solitude, delighted by the taste and texture of the coffee I've craved for so long. I open the morning paper and relax into the language, not because

I'm a woman alone who needs a barrier but simply because I want to read the news.

The midday meal is equally pleasant. Most days I take a break from my work around 2:30 PM, descending to the Prado's basement restaurant where prices are reasonable and the special of the day surprisingly good. There's fried cod with crisp potato slices, a version of *paella valenciana*, flan or rice pudding for dessert. As I eat, my notebook lies beside me on the table, a kind of companion, but my attention focuses on the scene around me, on the mannerisms and languages of fellow travelers. These are my people. We share a common purpose, and I don't mind eating alone among them.

It's in the evening that things get hairy. After the museum has closed and I've walked back to my hotel, rested and come back to life, I'm hungry in both body and spirit. I crave not just a meal, not just the take-out supper I can purchase in the supermarket of El Corte Inglés and carry to the emptiness of my room, but a complete dining experience. I want to move from bar to bar, sampling wine and tapas. I want a forkful of spicy *patatas bravas*, a few baked mushrooms, a couple of shrimp sautéed in garlic. I want to taste my way slowly to Puerta del Sol, working up to dinner in a place with atmosphere, with good music and lots of other people crowded together in the Spanish way, dressed up and enjoying a Friday night in Madrid.

But of course the Spanish way does not involve solitude. Friday night is for gathering together, for socializing in groups. Still, I tell myself, that's no reason for me not to enjoy a good meal. I think of my partner back in the States, how comfortable he is walking into a restaurant alone, developing an immediate friendly banter with the waiter, the bartender. If he were in my place right now, he'd focus only on finding a restaurant that would please him, not on how he might appear to other people when he entered.

For a long time I wander the streets searching for the right combination: interesting food, an inviting atmosphere, a table where I'll feel neither conspicuous nor isolated. At one point I follow the aroma of roasted garlic down an alley to a patio where contemporary flamenco music sets the mood. Outdoor seating can be perfect for dining alone if there's enough to look at on the street, but the patio tables are full at this restaurant, and everyone inside seems so young and trendy that I exit again and keep walking. A block later I stop and give myself a talking-to. This is ridiculous, I think. Just figure out what you want to eat and march into a place. If you don't feel uncomfortable, others won't respond to you with discomfort. But why, I keep wondering, do I feel this way?

At my first job, waiting tables in a small restaurant when I was sixteen, I felt mortified by other people's hunger. Partly this was because I was shy and unqualified for the job, and partly it was because there is such heartbreaking vulnerability in hunger, such laying bare of the soul in asking for food. "I want . . ." people would say to me, "Please bring me . . ." and my face would color each time. Or maybe not each time, maybe only when the customer was alone, looked tired or downtrodden, carried him or herself in a way that made me want to respond with more tenderness than I knew how.

In those days, before it occurred to me that I might move about in the world completely alone, I often mistook solitude for loneliness, to which I responded in an emotional way. The sight of a single diner could make my eyes fill with tears. Or a woman entering a movie theater alone could provoke a devastating wave of what felt like sympathy. I'd have to close my eyes tight against the image of her finding a seat, gazing up at the screen, eager to take in its stories. Later, on the way out of the theater, I'd search for her, trying to imagine what it was like to cross over into another world for two hours and have no one with whom to process that experience on the way home.

Much later, when I discovered Roland Barthes' essay, "Leaving the Movie Theater," I started to understand those earlier responses. Barthes describes how, under the cover of darkness, the theater becomes an erotically charged space. People abandon themselves, sink down into submissive postures, their bodies slack and senses fully receptive. The theater becomes a "site of availability," he says, and I think the same is true for restaurants. There's a degree of exposure in both places, in our wide-eyed, open-mouthed desire laid bare, and this exposure seems all the more evident in a person alone.

Now, all these years later, I understand that alone doesn't mean lonely, that desire is itself a tremendous pleasure. Now I love going alone to the movies — in any town, any country. In the soothing darkness of a theater, the crowd's collective laughter and audible breaths of surprise allow for both solitude and community. But somehow this peace of mind still doesn't translate to restaurants. Perhaps at an outdoor table with an unending view of the sea, I might be able to channel the comfort of a theater. But inside a restaurant, where every other table is a closed set—two, four, five bodies forming a coherent whole, I feel vulnerable. Unless I show that I'm occupied by reading or writing, my table lacks boundaries. I'm on display, hungry, desirous and, although I hate to admit it, ashamed of that state.

Eventually I circle back to a Cuban restaurant whose menu caught my eye an hour ago. I can see from the door that the employees are Caribbean, and their status as foreigners welcomes me. I enter, shoulders squared, and smile at a caramel-skinned woman whose long dreadlocks are wrapped with a bright blue scarf. She asks whether I'm meeting someone, then scans the L-shaped dining room, mouth puckering. After a moment she decides on a table along the far wall near the kitchen, a peripheral space that's fine with me. Throughout my meal she'll bring tiny plates of samples for me to try, and periodically one of the many cooks will come to the kitchen door and offer a smile.

Red beans and rice, fried plantains, mango salsa—I order exactly the kind of food I'm in the mood for, along with a glass of rioja. The atmosphere is lovely: brick walls hung with small, colorful paintings, Caribbean jazz. It's the perfect place for this evening, I think, and yet I can't seem to settle in. With my journal and postcards tucked inside the bag at my feet, I feel tense and then annoyed because of it. I don't know what to do with my hands as I wait. Or with my gaze. Straight ahead is the kitchen, to my right are a dozen tables filled with animated conversation. I scan the room periodically, trying to take in the scene without seeming like a voyeur, but there's no middle distance where my eyes can comfortably rest. If someone were sitting across the table from me, I'd cast my glance around the room as often as I liked, returning again and again to the safety of my companion's face. Without that cover, I feel conspicuous. I don't want my gaze to be misunderstood. I'm not lonely, I'm not at all wishing for company. I am simply, and obviously, alone.

I think of the great traveler and food writer M. F. K. Fisher, who moved about so confidently in the world, especially during the period of grief following her husband's death. "Sometimes," she wrote, "I would go to the best restaurant I knew about, and order dishes and good wines as if I were a guest of myself, to be treated with infinite courtesy." I want to treat myself this way, as a guest, as someone entitled to a fine meal in an exceptional place. But I also remember Fisher's comment on a group of travelers who once urged her to dine with them: "probably they felt sorry for me, all alone: most people are so afraid of that for themselves that they assume it is the same for others." Although I'm no longer afraid of being alone, I understand the response my solitude might provoke in other people, and it's difficult—unbearable, really—to be the object of such pity.

Because I want to feel comfortable in this situation, I concentrate on behaving as if I do. I sip my wine, breathe slowly, angle my body casually to the side, away from the wall. The food comes and I eat at a leisurely pace, practicing composure. I will my face to relax and smooth the wrinkles I know are forming on my brow, all of which helps. But it also takes effort. I begin to sense that I'm not dining so much as performing myself dining, and I can't help wondering if this experience is ultimately worth the trouble.

Then, as always, something remarkable happens. After an hour of hyperconsciousness, I step back onto the street. It's 11:30 at night, still dinnertime on a Friday in Madrid, and the sidewalks are crowded with people. In front of me, women link arms as they stroll, and a couple of men laugh riotously, stepping into my path. "Perdón, señorita," one smiles, touching my arm in apology, and I smile back, tell him not to worry. There's an energy on the street that's particular to Spain: a sense that being out in the world, eating and drinking and dancing and feeling oneself part of the social fabric, is as important as anything else we do. I relax. My stomach is full. The spicy food and the wine have fortified me, and as I walk along—in the opposite direction from my hotel because the mood on the street carries me that way—I feel enlarged, expanded, and deeply satisfied.

I remember then the title of Barthes' essay, "Leaving the Movie Theater." It was the aftereffect he loved most, the coming out of hypnosis and re-entering the world, which seemed so different after his absence, so much crisper and more mysterious. My reward for dining in the kind of restaurant I craved tonight is this return to the street, this sense of languid energy, of having experienced something luxurious and at the same time vital. Now I do feel like a guest—in this country, this city, in my own life. I've reached the point of reflection where the experience of dining, along with all the other wonderfully solitary experiences of the day, are settling into my body, my memory. This is the moment I love most about traveling alone, when I'm quiet, observing, letting the ideas grow and fade, waiting to see what comes next.

Motion Sickness

n the middle of the night, at the center of Madrid, the hotel rumbles and groans like the belly of a whale. The whoosh of fast-moving water means a toilet flushing; the intermittent thrum of a drain must be someone brushing their teeth. These sounds are almost comforting, a reminder that I'm not the only person awake at this hour, that my solitude is both circumstantial and temporary. But they're also a reminder of how mobile the other guests are, how free to walk from bedroom to bathroom and back again, to bend and stretch and stoop, to lie down on one side until that's no longer comfortable, then turn over. Such a simple thing it is to roll one's body, and yet I'm not able to do it myself.

I'm paralyzed, I keep thinking, but that seems too dramatic. I've never believed people who claim immobility because of back pain. I've sympathized, but on some level I've always thought — you *can* move, you just don't want to because it hurts so much. I tell that to myself now, my mind urging itself to overcome the body splayed across this bed, arms out to the sides, feet dangling. Every few minutes I gather my energy and concentrate on wriggling my fingers, and each time they respond I tremble with relief. Then, emboldened, I think, *lift your arm*. But there's a black hole in the center of my spine, and while the little signals get through, the larger ones disappear into it. I think, *bend your knee, turn your head to the side*, but nothing happens. The situation is so absurd I want to reassure myself by laughing, but I manage only a whimpering hiccup. Tears leak from the corners of my eyes, dribble down my temples, and land in my ears. I can't believe I can't lift my hands to brush them away.

Staring at the pebbled white ceiling, I try to focus on the bright side. At least I have a double bed to sprawl on. My first room at this hotel, three nights ago, had a narrow bed, a window that opened into a tiny air shaft, and an odor that said my ceiling vent was connected to someone else's bathroom fan. The next morning I argued for a long time with the front desk clerk, who insisted there were no other rooms available. "But I booked in advance and this room is unacceptable," I told him in halting Spanish. The clerk's youthful face grew animated but he wouldn't give in until I delivered my ace in the hole: "Just because I'm a woman traveling alone does not mean you can stick me in a closet." By the time I returned from breakfast, my room had been reassigned, my bags had been carried upstairs to a breezy, sunlit space, and the clerk had made sure to give me a *cama matrimonial.*

Now, pinned to this double bed like a moth in a specimen case, I think about the irony. I got what I wanted, and I'm stuck here. My room is on the seventh floor. The elevator goes as far as the fifth floor, after which a broad staircase takes over. That had seemed a charming quirk two days ago, and as recently as this morning I didn't mind the exercise. But when my back started to ache, then throb, then pulsate in a way that made it hard to breathe, the stairs became instruments of torture. By then it was too late in the day to call a chiropractor, so I dragged myself out to a pharmacy with visions of Vicodin dancing in my head. Doctors' prescriptions aren't necessary for most drugs in Spain, and I thought I'd be fixed up in no time at all. Instead, the pharmacist extolled the powers of anti-inflammatory medicine and sent me off with the largest ibuprofen tablets I've ever seen. On the excruciating climb back to my room, I consoled myself by thinking that even without a happy buzz, after taking one of those pills and lying flat on my back for a while, I'd feel better.

Now, at 1:30 in the morning, I do not feel better. I feel so much worse, in fact, that I can't imagine how I'll get myself to the airport tomorrow morning for the long flight home. The only light in the room is the sad flicker of a television hanging on the wall to my right. I can't turn my head enough to see it, and because I pressed mute an hour ago, just before I lay down, I can't hear it either. The remote control rests on the bedside table, three feet away, beside the box of ibuprofen and half a glass of water. It's too soon to take another pill according to the instructions, but if I could only reach that box, I would take several. I concentrate and command my arm to rise up, but nothing happens. I'm marooned, stranded, trapped in a state of suspended animation. A traveler going nowhere.

"Traveler" is a term I associate less with distance, frequency, or exotic destinations than with a way of being in the world. "I have traveled widely in Roanoke, Virginia," Annie Dillard famously wrote. Thoreau similarly believed that a circle with a ten-mile radius offered a lifetime's worth of exploration. And in fourteenth-century England, John Mandeville composed an entire book about his world travels— including his visits to the lands of hermaphrodites and of headless men whose eyes rested between their shoulders—all without leaving home. It took a couple of centuries before readers understood that Mandeville was an imaginative traveler, cribbing much of his itinerary from Marco Polo and fabricating the rest. In the meantime, his work was so popular that even Columbus is said to have taken a copy with him to the Americas.

I, too, think of myself as a traveler not because of the places I've been but because of the imaginative effect they have on me. When I'm on a trip, my memory goes into overdrive, trying to take in and store all kinds of impressions. I love being destabilized, seduced, made to fall in love with details I couldn't anticipate—the slant of sunlight over the industrial port of Hamburg, iguanas scattering like squirrels in a Yucatán park, the subtlety of color in the stark plains of eastern Wyoming. Above all, I love feeling my vulnerability lessen as my store of experience swells and the foreign slowly becomes familiar. Or at least I *have* loved this. But now, as I stare at the ceiling and reflect on my life—because intense pain has a way of prompting reflections on one's life—it occurs to me that perhaps like John Mandeville, I'm not really cut out for travel.

The first time I left home, I was eighteen and the only member of my family to go abroad without military orders. I'd prepared for the trip for most of a year, waiting tables full-time around my college class schedule to pay for summer study in Spain. My parents were simultaneously horrified and impressed, wondering what possessed me and when I'd become so determined. I wondered that too. I'd grown up viewing travel as a tremendous indulgence, an exercise for the leisure class, and the decision to head off alone for six costly weeks along the

Mediterranean seemed foolhardy even to me. But it also seemed crucial, as if being the kind of person who did such a thing would change the contour of my future.

It did, although I discovered even before leaving that there was an emotional price for becoming that kind of person. As the departure date neared, my hands began to shake and I had trouble sleeping. In the days before take-off, my emotions alternated between manic excitement and the purest form of grief. I kept bursting into tears as I packed up and said my good-byes, because I could see that life would continue in my absence, that my friends would occupy their time without me, that my bed would lie there unused, my scent slowly fading from its sheets. It was so easy to imagine my space in the world filling in that I began to fear I wouldn't return, that I'd perish somewhere between here and there, wherever there might be.

It's always tempting to disparage our younger selves, to chuckle at the inexperience we've outgrown. But the truth is I haven't outgrown the trauma of departure. Before almost every trip I take, I face that same anguish, that same inability to fathom my existence beyond the point of waving good-bye. I no longer tremble and weep, but I do suffer physically, with headaches, indigestion, insomnia. When I was in my late twenties and preparing to move to Spain for a year, my gastrointestinal system all but shut down, and I developed a visible drumbeat in my left eye. And when I arrived in Madrid two weeks ago, both the digestive problems and the twitch were back, accompanying me like cranky old friends. The tremendous thrill of travel, of packing everything I need into one bag and unmooring myself from routine, always comes with physical reminders of how precarious a thing this life is.

Never more so than tonight. I've pulled muscles before, I've even had my back "go out" in a way that required medication and a couple days of bed rest. But the difference between then and now is the difference between a tickle in the throat and pneumonia. This pain is so pervasive, radiating through my torso with each inhalation, that I can't believe a muscle or even a slipped disk could be the culprit. Perhaps a cancerous tumor has grown along my spinal cord, blocking motor coordination. Or a rare brain disease is destroying neural pathways. Or some hyper-mutated form of tuberculosis—which might explain the stabbing sensation when I breathe—will finish me off by morning. Only something very dramatic can possibly account for the sensation at my core right now, which I sum up for myself in one word: broken.

In between long stretches of panic are calmer moments, when I recognize that my back has stabilized itself as protection against further injury. The body is smart that way, digging in its proverbial heels when the mind refuses to take care. Today's warnings were at first too subtle to heed. I didn't make a sudden move or bend over in a way that caused a twinge; there was no clear beginning to the pain. It was simply an ache that grew and deepened over several hours. As the clock ticks toward my scheduled departure, I can't help wondering if this pain, this paralysis, is a psychosomatic response to travel, further proof that I'm better suited to the idea of a journey than to the journey itself.

By 3:00 in the morning, I've managed to grasp a pillow and slowly pull it under the edge of my back, creating enough leverage to roll onto my side. Then, by scooting my torso forward an inch at a time, I've gotten hold of the ibuprofen box. It takes awhile to tear open the foil bubble and place a pill on my tongue, and I have to swallow carefully because the glass of water remains out of reach. But the pill goes down, and after a few minutes' rest, I reach for another.

Around me, people continue to get ready for bed, clattering shut the Persian blinds on the outside of their windows. It is Spain, after all, where staying up late — even during the week — can be remedied by a siesta the next afternoon. I remind myself that if I can get to the airport tomorrow, I'll be able to sleep for eight hours on the plane, but that's small consolation. I need to sleep now, to rest my muscles, to relax enough to be able to get out of bed in the morning. On a chair across the room, an impossible distance away, is my purse with a box of motion sickness pills inside, and I imagine all sorts of Lucy Ricardo schemes that would allow me to reach it. Since childhood I've suffered from nausea and dizziness whenever I ride in a car or a bus, and so travel involves a supply of pills that calm my stomach and, as a side effect, relax my mind. I know this medicine wouldn't help my back tonight, but it might help me sleep.

On the other hand, my mind is so revved up right now that it's hard to imagine anything short of narcotics helping. In this perfectly stationary position, I'm in full travel mode. I move back and forth across the Atlantic, from New York where I grew up to Iowa where I now live to the Mediterranean island of Mallorca where last week I spent a few days visiting my friends Yolanda and Norbert. The past, present, and future roll around inside me, and in this feverish state I keep returning again and again to this week's trip to Oviedo, a place that stirs up all the complex emotions of departure.

I took the six-hour bus north from Madrid, fighting the drowsiness of my medicine because I didn't want to miss anything—not a kilometer of the dusty highway through León, not the increasingly hilly landscape as we neared Asturias, and certainly not the long mountain tunnel that would, just at the point of claustrophobia, open into a landscape of jagged gray peaks and emerald pastures. In the years since I moved away from Oviedo, I've often imagined this return trip, and I wanted to enjoy every moment of the real version.

In *The Art of Travel*, Alain de Botton uses the phrase "anticipatory imagination" to describe how, before arriving in a new place, we imagine an idealized version of our destination as if it were a landscape painting, bucolic and quiet and still. Anticipatory imagination omits and compresses, leaving out the gas stations and power lines so that upon arrival the traveler may feel surprised and disappointed by reality. De Botton doesn't talk about the anticipatory imagination of returning to a place we've been before, but surely it exists, enhanced by the omissions and compressions of memory. In my case, though, I was so aware of the nostalgic feelings I have for Oviedo that I assumed the city wouldn't live up to the grandeur in my mind, that everything would seem smaller and shabbier, the way a childhood home sometimes does once we've grown up. My anticipatory imagination erred on the side of pessimism.

In fact, the opposite was true. As I walked from the bus terminal to the pensión where I'd reserved a room, I could see that Oviedo had grown and expanded, and that the recent process of restoring historic buildings and making the downtown more pedestrian-friendly had enhanced the city's beauty. At the same time, the atmosphere of Oviedo seemed entirely familiar—the warm, humid air, the pungent smell of tobacco coming from the open door of a café, the *sidrerías* where waiters poured long streams of hard apple cider by holding the bottles at shoulder level and the glasses by their hips. (The secret, I remembered, was not to aim the bottle but rather to catch the cider with the glass. And also to take off one's wristwatch before try-ing.) It was nearly 9:00 PM and the sidewalks were bustling with baby carriages, leashed dogs, groups of men and women strolling with inter-locked arms and clustered on corners, chatting. This was exactly the way I remembered autumn evenings in Oviedo, with fragrant air and a yellow-pink sky and, as happens everywhere in Spain, an impres-sive number of people relaxing in public. I felt like a happy ghost, haunting the streets of memory, finding them just as delightful now as they'd always been.

Still, it's difficult to return to a beloved place, where time's rushing presence is felt so acutely. This was especially true a few days ago, when I visited my former housemate. We had been out of touch for a long time, my letters to her going unanswered. Then a few months ago I tried again, sending a postcard that announced my impending trip. Lola responded immediately. In the intervening years, she'd married and moved out of town, and the people who had sublet her apart-ment hadn't forwarded her mail. Now, separated and living back in Oviedo with her baby, she couldn't wait to see me.

When I arrived, we hugged and kissed a quiet greeting because the baby was asleep, and Lola immediately took me on a tour. We went through the kitchen and living room, where the accoutrements of her new life—bottles drying in the sink, tiny sweaters folded neatly on a bookshelf—made time seem scarily tangible. But my tiny former bedroom looked the same, stark white and empty, since Lola's most recent housemate had just moved out. It was thrilling to see the ar-moire, the wide window that looked out on a clothesline suspended five stories above the ground, the single bed in which I'd slept so well. And what pleasure it gave me to peer into the bathroom with its com-forting blue tile. I'd spent long hours lounging in the tub, listening to snippets of conversation from other apartments—a mother scold-ing a child, the man upstairs talking on the phone. I enjoyed soaking in a space that was alive with language and drama and the everyday workings of Spanish culture, and I especially enjoyed that none of the people around me knew I was listening, that I was there and not there all at once.

Over the midday meal, Lola and I talked in the same straight-forward way we always had. She told me about her marriage, her decision to leave her husband, what it was like to return to Oviedo as a single mother. I told her about graduate school, about the writing I was doing and the uncertain job prospects in my field. She patiently corrected my grammar, and when I said something that cracked her up, she covered her mouth with one hand and leaned forward to place the other hand on my shoulder as she caught her breath. It was a gesture I knew well, a gesture I had once described in an essay, and the accuracy of memory was so surprising that for a quick moment it seemed I'd written Lola into being.

Then, because she was enrolled in an afternoon computer class, a babysitter arrived, and we got ready to part once again. We took the elevator downstairs together, and Lola walked me "just one more block" several times, until she was already late for her class, and neither of us knew how to say good-bye and mean it.

Now, remembering that scene on the street, I can feel all the tension of departure throbbing in a muscle between my spine and my right shoulder. I imagine taking a razor blade and slicing into that muscle, then pulling the two sides apart and peering in. Like the scene in one of those water-filled globes, there would be Lola and I, walking in opposite directions down a sidewalk, turning to wave good-bye again and again, while the sparks from my nerve endings floated like silver snowflakes around us. And beneath that scene, layered deeper into the tissue, would be other scenes. My previous departure from Oviedo, for example, on a midnight bus to Madrid. Lola had driven me to the station with my huge, heavy suitcase, and I'd sent her away after a quick good-bye. The bus stood idling with everyone aboard except the driver, who'd gone for a cup of coffee, and I sat in the darkness, digging my fingernails into the palm of my hand. Suddenly there was a mad banging on the bus door and someone shouting my name. It was Lola's friend, Loli, to whom I'd said good-bye on the phone that afternoon because she had to work at night. I stumbled up the aisle as people craned their necks and stared; meanwhile, Loli went around to the driver's door and let herself in. Standing on the top step and leaning across the driver's seat, she stretched toward me, laughing. "I couldn't let you go without a hug!" she said, kissing my cheeks again and again, embracing me until the bus driver came up behind her shouting, "Hey! What do you think you're doing?" Deep inside the knots of muscle in my back are throbbing scenes like this one—dozens of them—that get to the most fundamental paradox of travel: at the moment of departure, I never want to go.

As proof of how difficult it is to leave places that mean a great deal to me, my body has clenched itself immobile. If I weren't in such agony, I might appreciate this gesture, pay attention to my physical determination to stay put for a while. Instead I panic, because the idea of lying in this room for another day or two, my body firmly anchored to the bed while my mind goes and goes, is unbearable.

In between its travels, my mind returns feverishly to the issue of my carry-on bag. When I packed up earlier, I wrapped two bottles of very good wine in layers of newspaper and placed them in my carry-on. One is for a friend, and the other is for the man with whom I've been involved for just a few months. On our first date we bonded over the discovery that at the same time I'd been living in Spain years ago, he'd been living next door in Portugal. As the conversation deepened, I confessed that I'd gone to Spain to flee a difficult relationship, and he said he'd gone to Portugal for the opposite reason, but he enjoyed his life in Lisbon so much that when the relationship ended, he stayed on for a couple more years. Right now he's at home in our small Midwestern city, stopping by my apartment each day to feed my cats. I want to thank him with the Portuguese wine I know he'll appreciate, and I can't stop fretting that even if I manage to get off this bed in a few hours, I'll never be able to lift my carry-on bag.

Another thing I'm fixated on is why I didn't stay in Oviedo longer. The university had wanted to extend my contract for a second year, had even offered to throw in some research work for additional salary, and Lola would have been thrilled to have me stay. I could have continued to live my relaxed existence, growing more fluent in the language, becoming fully acclimated to the culture. I wish now that I had done that. But I also remember that by the end of a year in Spain, I felt completely full. Full of language and experience and impressions of myself in a context I couldn't yet understand. As much as I wanted to stay in Oviedo, I also longed to consider my life there from a distance, to digest and make use of the lessons I'd learned—about identity, desire, how to be in the world. I wanted to look back on this time and begin to understand what it meant.

For a similar reason, I left Oviedo four days ago when I could just as easily have stayed a couple more days. Even before I arrived there last week, I already looked forward to leaving, to riding down the highway toward Madrid, watching the landscape transform itself back into an arid plain, and thinking over my experience. Perhaps the only thing that allows me to go through the pain of departure, again and again, is that once I'm away from a place, there's so much satisfaction in remembering it. But more than just memory is at work; travel invites a kind of recollective imagination, with all the compressions and omissions of de Botton's anticipatory form. Memory comes in snippets throughout the day and night, but recollective imagination is sustained, taking us back to the physical details of a place—the pungent smells of a city street, the thick flavor of hazelnut ice cream, the sound of a summer rain beating down on poplar trees in the corner of a park.

Recollective imagination is the prize for having traveled, for having gotten to a place and away again, more or less safely. How often a trying journey prompts the traveler to think, "At least this will make a great story." We console ourselves with the promise of remembering, of taking our story apart and putting it back together again, lingering in certain places and fast-forwarding in others. It's the fast-forward part I'm clinging to right now, the future perspective from which a night of full-body paralysis may not seem so bad.

At 7:30 AM, the alarm goes off. I've been dozing for two hours, falling into dreams between gunshots to the spine. Now I reach my arm carefully toward the clock and press the button until silence takes over the room.

Gingerly I wiggle my fingers and toes, then inhale until my lungs expand farther than I thought possible. I press my palm to the mattress and lift my torso slightly. The pain catches and I go down again, but after a moment I'm able to bring my knees up toward my stomach. I press the mattress with my palm once more and groan through the stabbing sensation. Once I'm seated upright, it isn't too hard to stand. There's no question the ibuprofen has worked its magic.

It takes an hour for me to dress, brush my teeth, and gather my toiletries. Then I kneel on the floor, repacking my suitcase in slow motion so that the two bottles of wine are deep inside it, cushioned by clothes. By the light of day, my mind is calm, reasonable, determined. My carry-on bag is still too heavy to lift, so I remove my wallet and passport and place them, together with the remaining ibuprofen tablets, in a light purse. Then I leave the room, shuffling like Methuselah toward the staircase. By holding the railing and using gravity to my advantage, wincing and gasping and breaking into a sweat, I make it down two flights. The elevator doors look for all the world like a finish line.

At the front desk, I confess to the clerk — the very same clerk I argued with a few days ago — that I cannot lift my bags. His face shows only concern as he dispatches a bellhop to retrieve my things and load them into a taxi, and I feel so relieved to be mobile, up and about and sure to catch my plane, that my eyes tear up when I say good-bye.

In Madrid, 9:15 AM is the early side of rush hour. As the taxi glides along the highway I think about how I'm leaving Spain again, this country that suits me so, with no idea when I might return. Regret and relief swirl together, making my head dizzy, my stomach tight. The sensation grows at my core until I finally realize that in all my careful preparations this morning, I forgot to take a motion sickness pill. I open the window slightly, lean my head back and close my eyes, trying to breathe. John Mandeville had the right idea in making it all up.

Travel is one of the most exhilarating and deeply disturbing things I do. Tomorrow I'll wake in my own bed, shaking with joy because help will be just a whisper away if I need it, and because this whole awful episode will be past tense. For a couple of weeks I'll feel so traumatized by last night that I won't be able to remember the details. I'll only know that I really and truly could not move. But then time will pass and the process of omission and compression and expansion will begin. Eventually, as so often happens with memory, I'll grow fond of the paralysis I once suffered, even suspicious that it could have been so complete. I'm not cut out for travel, it's true. But I've become the kind of person who does it anyway, ignoring the motion sickness, suffering through departure, and looking forward, each time, to the pleasure of having been.

Authenticity and Artifice

magine. The year is 1868. The location is a small village in northern Spain, a day's journey west of Santander and five kilometers south of the Cantabrian Sea. The time is just before sunrise, when the dark sky above this region of mountains and farmland turns pale as chalk, and the yellow stone buildings of Santillana del Mar begin to glow.

In the early light, a man named Modesto Cubillos ambles through town, the wooden heels of his boots scraping along cobblestone. A large leather pack rests against his hip, the strap of a shotgun crosses over his chest. In front of him trots a dog, nose to the ground, moving as its master does, without hurry. They pass through the Plaza de las Arenas, alongside the collegiate church where the martyred bones of Santa Juliana rest, and into a narrow street of seventeenth-century houses leaning against one another like confidantes. When the houses give way to pasture, the man turns onto a trail toward the southern hills and the dog, having stopped to investigate some horse droppings, runs to catch up.

The autumn air is mild and moist, the grass shimmers with dew. Modesto Cubillos hums quietly as they climb, rising above the fields and farmhouses, above the landscape shrouded in a thin mist. Within half an hour's time they reach the top of a ridge, where Cubillos pauses to admire the Picos de Europa in the distance, their snowcaps gleaming under a new sun.

Then, something amazing happens: the dog sniffs its way to a brush-filled depression in the hillside and disappears. Cubillos whistles, calls out, walks the length of the thicket and back again, puzzled. He sinks to his knees for a better look, then opens his pack and removes a pair of leather gloves. He stomps and tears at the brush, making his way into the area where the dog vanished. A few meters in, he discovers a mess of broken-up rock in front of what looks like a gash in the hillside. He approaches, whistling again for the dog, and discovers an opening large enough to step through.

Imagine. It's fully daylight by now, but he can't see inside. What does he do? Does he push ahead, impetuously? Or does Modesto Cubillos wait for the dog to come out again, happy in its doggy discoveries, before he becomes the first person in recorded history to enter this cave?

On a glorious mid-summer morning, I ascend the hill toward Altamira, walking on a cement path alongside the road. From the guest house where I'm staying in Santillana del Mar to the top of this ridge is only supposed to take half an hour, but I'm walking slowly, enjoying the hot sun, and keeping an eye out for anything that might seem familiar. I pass the last of the inns and farmhouses, their side yards populated with cows and roosters and a single horse that leans against a fence, blinking away flies. Now the land beside this path falls rapidly away, into a valley of cultivated fields that curve up and over a distant hillside. What feels like memory stirs inside me, but I'm not sure whether to trust it.

Near the top of the ridge, the path crosses over the road, ducks behind a stone wall, and becomes a wide dirt trail that continues up the hill. Not far along this stretch, I see an older man walking toward me. Even before he's close enough for a greeting, a bloody gouge the size of a thumbprint announces itself on his forehead, just above where his hairline might once have been. "¡Buenos días!" he calls cheerily. I respond in kind, stealing glances at the wound.

"The path is closed up there," he says, extending his arm and pointing. "The workers gave me a terrible time about getting through. You should take the road instead." I quickly scan his body, looking for evidence of a fall, but his khaki trousers and pressed linen shirt are clean. Perhaps he scraped his head on a tree branch, or maybe the injury happened days ago and is healing slowly. I can't think of a polite way to ask.

The man's face is fleshy and smooth, adorned with a gray mustache and framed by short white hair. "Imagine," he tells me brightly. "The last time I was here was sixty years ago. How different it was then! We had to bring our own flashlights into the cave in order to see anything. Sixty years ago."

"That's a long time," I reply, and he nods. "I'm eighty-five years old. I was a student in Santander then. My father and a friend of his picked me up and we came here to explore. Sixty years ago." He looks out over the stone wall toward the valley, and the sunlight shining on his head captures the orange tint of Mercurochrome.

I ask whether he's visited the new museum this morning. "*Claro*," he says, pulling a ticket stub from his pocket and holding it out to me as proof. "Oh it's a very good reproduction. The paintings especially are very, very good. Of course, it's not the same as seeing the ones inside the cave itself. How could it be? I saw the real paintings sixty years ago. With my father. He's been dead now nearly that long."

He loops through the story again and again. I wonder if he fears I don't understand, or if he just enjoys rehearsing the details. It was his father's friend who came up with the idea, and the two men picked him up in Santander. They had to bring their own flashlights. His father died not long after. And now, at eighty-five years old, he's walked two kilometers uphill to return to a cave it's no longer possible to enter.

I tell him that I, too, once entered the cave, that I've come here now to compare the paintings in the replica with the ones in my memory. The man nods solemnly. Then he leans toward me, his face guileless as a boy's. "I remember the cave," he confesses. "But the truth is I don't remember the paintings inside. I try, but there's nothing there." He shrugs, then stares at me, eyes wide, and I can see that he's back inside Altamira, craning his neck and holding up a light, searching.

Imagine, the tour guide had said. Fourteen thousand years ago, the Iberian Peninsula was ten degrees cooler than it is now. Here in the north of Spain there were dense forests, tall grasslands, abundant wildlife. Bison, deer, goats, boars with giant tusks roamed this very hillside. During the Lower Magdalenian period, people hunted with elaborate stone tools and lived primarily in caves. And some of them were artists. Their creations survive in many forms, from rock carvings to decorated spears, but none are as impressive as the paintings inside Altamira.

On a clear spring day, twenty of us stood on a hillside overlooking a patchwork of farmland that rolled across a valley and up a ridge, disappearing into the perfect blue sky. White houses with orange tiled roofs clustered together between the fields, and slightly to the north we could make out the crowded rooftops of Santillana del Mar. Five kilometers beyond that village lay the rocky seashore, and I tried to wrap my mind around the news that 14,000 years ago, before the end of the last glacial age, that shore had been an additional five kilometers away.

Imagine, the guide said, and I tried. I was used to visiting historical sites, cathedrals and sepulchers and the mountaintop from which Pelayo launched the Reconquest. I loved living among evidence of the past and using it to imagine my way back in time. But this much time was impossible. Reaching into dimmest memory, I could fabricate pictures of Ancient Rome, Ancient Greece, the earliest cities of Mesopotamia. But that still left a 10,000-year gap between the remotest, sketchiest bit of history I'd absorbed and the people for whom Altamira was home. I squinted until the farmhouses and hedgerows disappeared, until the fields waved with tall grass, my vision based largely on the opening of *2001: A Space Odyssey*.

It was a privilege to be here. Only a small number of people were allowed into the cave each day, and the waiting list for admission was three years long. But a friend of mine had petitioned to bring a group of international scholars to Altamira, and his persuasive argument was approved in less than a year. At first I declined his invitation to go along, since I knew nothing about Paleolithic art and didn't want to bump someone else from the tour. But Enrique insisted this wasn't an opportunity to miss, that the cave would be closed to the public one day soon. And anyway, he said, by "international scholars" he really just meant some friends from the university, foreign students and teachers like me, almost none of whom knew anything about this cave.

The guide was onto us from the first moment. Probably she'd been expecting anthropologists and art historians, people whose enthusiasm for Altamira would match their understanding of what they were about to see. Instead, she got a motley group of folks who were trying hard to look informed, furrowing our brows and nodding intensely at her explanations. I gazed out at the cloudless sky, deeply blue above us and paler toward the horizon, and tried to imagine standing in this very place, peering through the tall grass, long before hours and minutes and millennia existed. I didn't know how else to *be* in a place like this, and at the same time my imagination lacked fuel. So I grabbed at provocative details—that a rock fall had closed the cave 13,000 years ago, that it had remained hidden until the middle of the nineteenth century, when blasting at a nearby quarry jarred the rocks loose. That in 1868 a hunting dog had serendipitously led its owner inside.

"By now you might be wondering where the cave is, exactly," the guide said, as if she hadn't uttered these words dozens of times before. She pointed downward, flexed her knees as if pushing into the ground. "Just nine meters below where we stand is the Sistine Chapel of Paleolithic Art."

Naturally Modesto Cubillos told people about his discovery. Why not? It was a cave, a hidden world where rooms and passageways stretched for 270 meters into the earth. Of course people cleared away the brush and rocks and began to enter. Not a lot of people at first, mostly shepherds who ducked in during rainstorms, but eventually word reached Marcelino Sanz de Santuola, a local landowner fascinated by the new science of archaeology. In the cave's large vestibule Santuola discovered arrows made of flint, the charred remains of a fire, animal bones and hair. Deeper in the interior, in the dangerously narrow "horse's tail," he discovered elaborate carvings on the walls. He didn't know what to make of all this until a few years later, when he attended the Paris World Exposition and saw Paleolithic artifacts on display. As soon as possible he returned to Altamira, wisely bringing along his eight-year-old daughter, María.

Imagine. María is a studious girl with short, light-brown hair and a serious expression. She's thrilled to be exploring a cave alongside her father, searching for treasure. Santuola kneels beside his lantern in the cave's vestibule, scooping dirt and examining it closely, looking for tiny shards of flint. He's whistling a little under his breath, the way he always does when he concentrates. María squats nearby, beside the soft glow of her own lantern, also looking at the dirt. She's fantasizing about finding something very important, something that would please her father and impress the children of Santillana del Mar. She's rocking back on her heels, eyes following the lamplight up over the wall of the vestibule and then back along the ceiling into the next chamber. She's searched the floor of that chamber already, but now, as her eye traces the ceiling, she notices something else. María stands and steps toward the second chamber, holding her lantern before her, intrigued. At the entry to that long, low room she tilts her head all the way back and exclaims, "Look Papá! Oxen!"

A splash of red so brilliant the paint seems wet. Charcoal lines curving flawlessly over rock. A bison poised to leap from the ceiling, its muscles taut under shimmering hide, tail raised and curled. On the Great Panel, twenty-seven bison gallop, lie down, stand gazing backward into the herd. Some of the images require patience, a Rorschach test for the collective unconscious, while others spring immediately to life. One animal leans forward slightly, neck extended and head raised, bellowing with such force that my mind instantly supplied the sound. I inhaled sharply and took a step back.

The painter also had the talent of a sculptor, taking advantage of a rugged, bulging canvas. A shoulder swells with the limestone, a belly curves into a recess, indentations in the rock give depth to an eye. I couldn't believe that the human mind 14,000 years ago—a mind that hadn't found its way to, say, the wheel—understood not only color and shading but dimension as well.

The guide explained that a single artist created all twenty-seven of the bison, mixing iron oxide with water for the paint and burning pine boughs for charcoal. At least three colors of paint were used, and the charcoal strokes were made by a confident hand, with no corrections, no scraping away of lines that didn't work. Remarkably, although the bison range in size and activity, they share the same proportions. "The artist painted from memory," the tour guide said, drawing our attention to what should have been obvious. Of course there had been no models, no photographs of bison to work from, no possibility of peering outside from the depths of the Polychrome Chamber to watch an animal stroll across a hillside. There had only been memory and imagination, those amazing twin powers of the human mind.

The guide asked us to note how many bison there were, in how many different poses, and yet none of them overlapped. Some covered much earlier paintings, but they never infringed on one another. The space was used with perfect economy. "And look here," she said, leading us deeper into the chamber. "This one is much older, dating back perhaps 2,000 years before the others. See the difference?" I did see, and my heart leapt at the two-dimensional outline of a pygmy horse.

That was what I'd expected to find here, a simplistic representation of the complex world outside, something closer to what I might have drawn if I'd lived at that time, seen what this person had seen, felt compelled for whatever reasons to recreate the image inside a cave.

Closer to the door of the chamber, the guide again trained her flashlight. I heard a gasp from the front of the group and waited my turn as people looked, smiled, nodded their heads, then filed back out into the vestibule. When I finally stepped forward, I saw the faint image of another horse and then, just above it, the ghostly red imprint of a human hand. Instinctively, my own hand raised itself up in the gesture of a wave.

After the rock slide closed the cave—remarkably with no one inside—the temperature in Altamira remained a constant fifty-seven degrees, the humidity 87 percent. No bacteria grew on the limestone, no light faded the colors of the paint. Over the next several thousand years, as the earth underwent a climate shift that caused warmer temperatures and a scarcity of large game, people adapted from a nomadic, hunter-gatherer existence into a more settled, agricultural lifestyle. Inside the cave, though, none of these changes were apparent. When María de Santuola looked up and saw the bison, when her father rushed to her side and felt the blood drain from his face, the paintings may have looked very much the same as when their creator stepped outside and wiped a color-stained hand in the grass.

Santuola studied the paintings carefully, comparing them and other objects from the cave with documented Paleolithic remains. In 1780, he published his conclusions in a modestly-titled book, *Brief notes on some prehistoric objects from the province of Santander*, to which the academic community responded with derision. Scholars declared the paintings frauds because they were too accomplished and too well-preserved; one went so far as to accuse Jesuit priests of commissioning the paintings in an attempt to undermine the theory of evolution. If the human mind could create such astonishing work so long ago, the argument went, there wasn't much to evolve from.

Santuola was undeterred by the criticism. In a move that greatly helped conserve the paintings, he paid to have a door installed in the cave's opening and convinced the town council of Santillana del Mar to allow visitors inside only when accompanied by a municipal guide.

Gradually, over the next two decades, the academic world made its peace with Altamira as more and more prehistoric artifacts were discovered across Europe. In 1902, some years after Santuola had passed away, a prominent historian apologized publicly for his earlier disbelief, subtitling his book about the cave *A Skeptic's Mea Culpa*.

Once word spread of the authenticity of Altamira, interest in the cave skyrocketed. Everyone from scientists to art historians to people who were merely curious came to explore. Because of blasts from the earlier rock quarrying, however, the cave's structure had become fragile, and frequent rock falls prompted the construction of concrete retaining walls, which drastically reduced the size of both the vestibule and the Polychrome Chamber. Later, as the number of visitors continued to increase, paths were smoothed out, stairs constructed, and electric lighting was added to assist the tours. And because the Polychrome Ceiling was so low, ranging from six feet in some places to just over four feet in others, the floor under the Great Panel was dug out to allow for a better view.

During the latter part of the twentieth century, Altamira became one of the top tourist destinations in Spain. In 1973 alone, 177,000 people entered the cave, an average of more than 500 visitors a day. As a result, body heat and carbon dioxide levels began to change the cave's atmosphere. Temperature and humidity increased, prompting bacteria to grow on the walls and ceiling and causing the paintings, after so many millennia, to begin to decay.

The tour guide explained most of this before we entered Altamira. She told us how in 1978 the Spanish government created the National Museum and Research Center of Altamira, which immediately closed the cave to the public and devoted the next three years to studying conservation. She made clear that we were part of the very small number of people who'd been allowed in since the cave reopened, and she predicted that soon, very soon, a replica of the cave would replace the real one as the main tourist attraction of this area. "In the future, we hope to protect the paintings from the destruction we humans cause every time we go inside the cave," she said, and we bowed our heads, nodding with guilt, thrilled beyond measure at our good fortune.

Heeding the elderly man's warning, I ascend the last 200 meters to Altamira on the thin shoulder of the road, cringing each time a car speeds by. Then I purchase a ticket in a small building alongside the parking lot and head directly for the entrance to the original cave. I'm excited to visit the new museum, but what I want more than anything is to return to a place I've already been, to loiter before a thick door in a hillside, then ascend further and compare the view above the cave with the one that's been fading in my memory for a dozen years. I want to stand there, close my eyes, feel time folding in on itself so that the person I once was and the person I am now will seem for a moment indistinguishable.

This, I imagine, was the elderly man's wish as well. But as I soon discover, the trails that snake over the hillside are cordoned off because of construction, and a guard informs me that no one can walk near the cave entrance or on the ridge above it until the project is complete. It will be this way all summer, he insists, no exceptions. With several other tourists, I stand at the edge of the prohibited zone, staring at the grassy trail leading into a clump of trees and brush. The cave entrance is just out of view, and I curse under my breath at the bad timing.

The hillside is so green, so lush, so inviting. How I long to walk there and there and way up there, where I could gaze out toward the Picos de Europa to the south. Consumed with disappointment, I wander as far as the ribbons will allow, toward the construction site that is slightly downhill from the cave. Then I realize that the path I'm on is still open, that it skirts the site and heads downhill to where I met the man. If the workers gave him a hard time about getting through, he must have been wandering in the restricted area. He must have ignored the warning signs, stepped over the ribbon, and gone to see what he could see.

This pleases me greatly. I'm tempted to do the same thing myself, despite the lurking guard. That's how magnetic an attraction authenticity has, how much the physicality of place promises. Being there, even when *there* is a door we can't walk through, enhances the imaginative part of memory until we can feel the past in our cells. The desire to return—to the beginnings of experience, to places that help us grasp the concept of time—is a powerful motivator. Perhaps my friend hoped to find some detail that would stir his memory, take him back to an earlier version of himself, in the company of his father, on a day when the future seemed as sublime and unending as the view. Perhaps he wanted, as I do, to sneak up and explore the sealed entrance of the past.

The new museum complex at Altamira opened in 2001. Using the latest digital technology, a team of engineers and artists mapped every micro-millimeter of the cave's vestibule and Polychrome Chamber, then created a replica to scale, using resin and crushed limestone. Each bump and fissure of the walls and ceiling are accounted for, and because of advanced studies into pigmentation and flat-hand application techniques, artists were able to reproduce the paintings to perfection. Now, up to 200,000 visitors each year can examine the bison, along with many of the older animals and engravings, including some from parts of the cave that were never open to the public.

Creating the "neo-cave" at Altamira wasn't just a matter of reproduction. In planning, its designers considered the truth of the space they wanted to build. There was no need to replicate the current condition, the artificial supporting walls, pathways, and stairs. Why not instead build a version truer to the Altamira of the Lower Magdalenian era? The cave's entrance could be returned to its fifteen-meter-wide state, as it had been before the first rock fall. The vestibule could take on the size and shape it was when humans lived inside, allowing daylight to reach nearly to the Polychrome Chamber. In short, the replica could allow visitors an experience that was in some respects more authentic and more conducive to the imagination than the real cave just a short distance away.

Long before arriving at the new museum, I read about its ecological design, about how little the building interrupts the hillside on which it stands. Even so, I'm surprised by how effortlessly the long, low roof and ocher façade meld into the grassy slope. As museums go, it doesn't look like much from the outside. But as a respectful invasion into the landscape, it impresses me greatly.

The meeting place for tours of the neo-cave is in a roped-off area of the lobby. Entrance tickets come with a time stamped on them, and mine is ten minutes away. I watch as a woman in the navy blue suit of a docent greets the 12:30 PM group, watch as a piece of the wall they're standing beside slides open and swallows them up. My stomach tightens with nervous energy, the way it does when I'm waiting to meet someone at an airport, scanning the faces coming through the arrivals gate for one that's familiar. This is the way I might have felt before visiting the original cave if I'd studied anthropology or archaeology, if I'd known then what Altamira had to offer.

Now I do know. In the years since my first trip here, in the process of trying to understand why my experience in the cave has come back to me so often, carrying me without warning to that bright May morning, that first glimpse across more time than I know how to process, I've prepared fully for my return. I've researched not only the real cave and its paintings but the history of conservation at Altamira, the construction of the neo-cave, the lifestyle of Lower Magdalenian people. There's nothing this tour guide will tell me, I think boldly as I step into the roped-off area, that I don't already know. That cocky thought turns out to be true. But it's also the case that this tour of Altamira may have less to do with knowledge than with imagination.

First, a video viewing room. A timeline of human history, a group of actors with hippy-long hair and smudged faces moving in and around a cave. Then, a corridor opening into the neo-cave. On the left, a glass wall fifteen meters wide, beyond which lies the breathtakingly real scene of grass, trees, distant blue hills, a vast sky. Straight ahead, a hearth, the ground beside it littered with tools and the remains of a carcass. As we gather around, a hologram of a family appears, a ghostly version of a mother, father, and son all working to prepare a meal.

Next, a series of ramps snake back and forth, leading us below ground. This area is not reproduced from the original, but halfway down, a simulated archaeological dig shows the two major occupations of the cave, 14,000–16,000 years ago and 18,000–21,000 years ago. A little further along, a replica of Paleolithic tools offers some details of the painting process.

And then, finally, we enter the Polychrome Chamber—a room so large and clean and well lit, with a painted ceiling so tall and pristine, it's like nothing I've ever seen before.

Ten minutes was all that had passed when we emerged from the real cave, blinking and yawning in the daylight. Inside, in the presence of such unexpected artistry, I'd been impressed and also troubled, made aware of the contours of my own ignorance. Now, at the moment when my visit shifted from experience to memory, I wished I'd dropped something inside, an earring or my watch, any excuse to rush back into the Polychrome Chamber and look harder, closer, with a greater sense of urgency.

Enrique thanked the guide in his charming way, and we walked toward the museum, my mind struggling to catch up with my body, the way it does with jet lag or culture shock. In the small, adjacent building there were display cases of arrows, timelines of human development, drawings that showed a Lower Magdalenian man dressed in sewn animal hides. I imagined this figure charring strips of pine and mixing the ash with earth and water, stirring the paint in seashells, in the kneecaps of bison. I imagined him kneeling where the ceiling was lowest and stretching where it was high, translating the picture inside his mind into three-dimensional form.

Most remarkable of all were the museum's photographs, in which the paintings appeared impossibly crisp. A shiver of recognition ran up my arms as I gazed at reproductions of what I'd witnessed just minutes before, in a better light than the cave provided. Without photographic illumination, without lying on the floor and using a wide-angle lens, you simply couldn't see the paintings inside the cave as they appeared here, the subtle changes in color, the tiny etchings that give texture to the animals' hides. Looking at the pictures, I felt the already fading images in my mind becoming more complex, more brilliant, more worthy of awe than they'd been a little while ago. The truth of my own experience was already changing.

The most disconcerting thing about the neo-cave is not the artifice of it, not the lighting or the multi-media displays but the number of visitors. Our tour has fifteen people, and there are four other groups inside, stopping at the various displays. The guides' voices echo, intertwining with one another so that I can't seem to isolate what ours is saying. I ask a question about proportions—is the distance between the vestibule and the Polychrome Chamber the same here as it is in the real cave? I want a simple yes or no, but the woman offers a lengthy response I can't begin to decipher.

And so, two days later, I return yet again to Altamira. I come late in the afternoon, when I hope there will be fewer people, and buy a ticket for the last available entrance time. I stand behind the roped-off area with a German couple and two Spanish men, fidgeting until the wall opens up and I see that our guide is someone new. She smiles in what seems to be a genuine way, perhaps relieved that the end of a long week is near.

We watch the video, step into the neo-cave, gather before the hologram. There is only one tour group ahead of us, so the replica is wonderfully quiet, and I understand everything the guide says. When I ask about the distance between the vestibule and the Polychrome Chamber, she says it's exactly the same as in the original. I ask about the tools around the hearth, about the clothing and language of the people in the hologram, anything to slow her down and let the other group complete its tour. She seems happy to oblige.

In the Polychrome Chamber, we linger over details of the bison. The German couple doesn't speak Spanish, so the guide uses a laser pointer and some pantomime to explain what we're looking at, and I translate a few words into English for them. I ask how much higher this ceiling is than the real cave, and the guide points to a line halfway up the wall. "That's where the original floor was. But of course, even in the real cave, the floor was lowered to help people see better."

I imagine all of us standing where that line on the wall is, so close to the ceiling we could reach up and lay our palms flat against it, as the artist did when applying the paint. I imagine dimmer lighting, shadows, the smell of condensation on soil and stone, and I imagine María de Santuola looking up, delighted by the color. Suddenly, for a brief, illusory moment I'm back in the cave, head tilted, that first glimpse of bison nearly overpowering me. Surprised and exhilarated by the sensation, I can't help blurting out, "I've been inside the real cave!"

The guide widens her eyes and smiles, though she must hear this often. "Then you remember the rock," she says. "The gigantic rock underneath these paintings right here. You had to lie back against it and look up to see them. Remember?"

In a flash I'm in two places at once, here in this cavernous room and there, in the narrow passageway of memory where an enormous rock makes the Polychrome Chamber seem smaller than it is. Now it makes sense that my recollection of the paintings has always placed them not on the ceiling but on a wall directly in front of me. I can feel the cool, hard rock beneath my back, the muscles of my stomach tightening as I stand up once again. I'm not sure whether this memory is authentic or whether it's a product of suggestion, but it's inside me now in a permanent way.

What a slippery fish truth is. What a brilliant picture, constantly fading.

Between the Polychrome Chamber and the rear exit of the neo-cave, I pause and gaze up toward the opening. Being inside this replica is not at all like being inside the real cave. But from this vantage point, with the vast blue sky shining outside the wide entrance, I can almost imagine leaving the Polychrome Chamber, hands wet with paint, a sense of accomplishment pulsing along my spine, and stepping toward the brilliance of the real world outside.

A cave, a set of representations, themes of authenticity and truth — Plato is waiting on the sidelines, just itching to be brought in. In his cave, after all, prisoners were chained so that they saw only the representations, only the shadows moving along the cave's back wall. The prisoners couldn't turn their heads, so they didn't know that a fire burned behind them and that men walked back and forth before the fire, holding up images that created the shadows. All the prisoners saw were the shadows themselves. They named them, made up stories about them, devised games to predict which images would appear next. Plato's cave-dwellers were an imaginative crowd, in their own way.

The Parable of the Cave cautions against believing what we take in with our senses. Truth lies not in representations, Plato insisted, and not even in the source of the representations, but in a philosophical ideal we can only glimpse through logic and rigorous study. Plato was a philosopher, of course, writing after his beloved teacher, Socrates, was sentenced to death for the way his mind worked. Had Plato been an artist, had Socrates lived to a natural death, the parable might have gone another way.

Plato's allegory, with its cave-dwellers, its shadows, its eternal divide between observation and understanding is brilliantly captivating. Even for those of us who believe that truth lies not in a philosophical ideal but in the constant process of negotiating between memory and imagination, symbol and meaning, authenticity and artifice.

Here is the truth: When I close my eyes and concentrate in just the right way, I remember. A narrow passageway, a slightly uneven floor, dim lighting. And then, suddenly, a burst of color so bright I took a step back. I remember the flank of a bison, the charcoal shading, the russet color of the hide. "My God," I said in Spanish, in a tone of unpleasant surprise. I remember the dim lighting, the bright color, the flank. I remember my strange response. I remember feeling grateful for the outline of a horse. And I remember the small, stunning imprint of a human hand. When I close my eyes and concentrate, I catch glimpses of that day, of the cool, damp air on my skin, the uneven floor beneath my shoes. The dim lighting, the flank, the horse, the hand. In sixty years these, too, will be gone.

The replica ends with the Polychrome Chamber, but the hallway outside is lined with panel reproductions from the cave's tail. In the real cave, this is the very narrow space that stretches deep into the earth, the area where none but the most specialized scientists are allowed. Our guide points out some carvings, geometric shapes etched into the limestone, and then she focuses on the masks. I'd seen them on the tour two days ago, and I remember the guide in the real cave describing them to us. Human faces carved in key spots where, it's assumed by anthropologists, they played a role in spiritual rituals.

"But the curious thing," the current guide says, "is that in the real cave you don't see the masks as you walk into the tail. You only see them when you turn around and come back out. The faces are pointed toward the deepest, darkest part of the cave."

We accept that information, nodding. The Germans don't understand, the Spanish guys are already leaning toward the exit, and I, too, am finished with this tour. In my mind, I'm walking back down the hill toward town, taking a seat at an outdoor table, and ordering a glass of red wine. I'm ready to enjoy the memory of this tour and the links it offers to my previous experience. I'm happy as can be, delighted with myself for coming back at this time of day and delighted with the tour guide for her clear, attentive speech.

But she isn't finished yet. She's looking me right in the eye, an astonished smile on her face. "Why?" she's saying. "Why would they have carved the faces in that direction? What purpose could these images have served?"

Not sure whether it's a rhetorical question, I respond, "I don't know."

She laughs. "No one knows! And we'll never be able to know. Isn't it marvelous? All we can do is imagine. But the people who put them there—*they* knew." The guide isn't frustrated by ignorance, by our collective inability to turn our gaze behind us and see the truth of this place. Instead, her voice is textured with pleasure and awe, and it's that sound more than anything—more than the reproduced paintings or carvings or the fabulously wide new entrance—that makes me feel I've been inside the cave today. It's the thrill in her voice, in the gorgeous mystery of all that time folding up between us, in the questions we'll forever be trying to answer.

After leaving the museum at Altamira that first time, after walking back down the grassy slope in the sun, we international scholars boarded a bus and rode to the coastal town of Ribadesella. There, we sat down at an outdoor café, twenty of us clustered around four or five tables, the sun warming our arms and necks, and I ordered a glass of sweet vermouth, which impressed the Spaniards among us. For a long time we sat and basked and no one said anything. I was remembering being inside the cave, its darkness, its chill, and thinking even then that I might have lived my entire life without going there, without knowing about Altamira, which wouldn't have been such a terrible thing. But now I wouldn't live that way, and it pleased me.

I was remembering being inside the cave, but already the memory was fading, making space for future impressions, for facts and stories and the imaginative project of recollection. Ten minutes is time enough only to glimpse, to step back in awe, to hold a hand up and sense through the palm, up the arm and along the spine, the gossamer thread of connection. Afterwards, experience begins.

The Impossible Overcome

Afterwards, on the train to Bilbao, a man at the back of the car will sit bellowing, his baritone voice somewhere between a song and a dirge.

Although I won't be able to see him, I'll know he is heavy-set, with rumpled clothing and dark, unwashed hair. I'll remember the way he sat near me on the platform in Guernica, intoning even then a litany of mundane information about today's date, how old his father is, the gray skies that promise rain. He seems to be in his mid-thirties. He is not carrying a bag or a backpack. I have no idea what these observations mean.

After a while it will be the silences that disturb me most, the moments in between, when I'm on edge waiting for him to start again. Outside the window, oak and pine forests pass by, broken now and then by a meadow, a farm, a village. At each station people will board and take their seats, unsuspecting. Then the train will press forward, and I'll watch their shoulders tighten in response to a voice that swells from behind like a threat. Or a warning. Or a haunted, recurring memory.

In the Basque language, it's spelled *Gernika*.

Euskara, the language of the Basque region of Spain, is said to be nearly impossible to learn. Legend has it that the devil himself, after realizing that no Basques had ever gone to Hell, eavesdropped for seven years in hopes of mastering the tongue. But eventually he gave up, having understood only three words and all of them curses.

As the co-official language of Biscay, Euskara appears first on street signs, maps, and brochures. The Spanish translation appears right below, but I have trouble focusing on it with the Basque *k*'s and *x*'s and *tz*'s seducing my eye. I don't know how to pronounce the intriguing combinations of letters or which syllables to stress, so I can't practice saying the words. This shouldn't matter since only 25 percent of the people who live in this region speak Euskara, and as I travel there's no pressure to say even "hello" or "thank you" in that language. But nothing entices as much as what you can't get near. Everywhere I go, the beguiling secrets of Euskara remind me how much I don't know, how much I can't even imagine.

Until recently I didn't know Guernica still existed, or rather that it existed *again*, after being leveled in a 1937 bombing raid. And I didn't know it's been the symbolic center of *Euskai Herria*—the land of Basque speakers—since the Middle Ages. All I knew was that Picasso's mural about the horrors of war had made the town synonymous in my mind with tragedy. When I came across Guernica in a guidebook listing of worthwhile places in the Basque country, I was immediately intrigued. It's located an hour outside Bilbao, where I'm staying for a few days, and train access couldn't be easier. Although being a tourist through horror makes me feel uneasy, like a voyeur, I wake up on a cool July morning eager to visit the source of Picasso's inspiration.

The first time I encountered *Guernica* I was eighteen years old and nearing the end of a summer study abroad program. On an August afternoon, as our tour wound slowly through the Prado's magnificent, crowded halls, I felt overwhelmed, privileged, and impatient to see what I'd come for: Goya's twin paintings of *La Maja*—a woman reclining on a couch, fully clothed in one scene and comfortably naked in the next. The previous year a college professor had shown slides of the paintings, and I'd fallen in love with them, with the wry half-smile of the clothed woman, with the slight relaxation of her eyes and lips in the nude. It was because of those paintings that I'd scraped together enough money to spend six weeks studying in Spain, and when we finally reached the third floor room where the images hung side by side, I started to cry. Because they were smaller, more delicate, more beautiful than I'd imagined. Because I was right there, standing in front of them.

Afterwards, we went to the Casón del Buen Retiro, the annex of the Prado that housed *Guernica*, where I did not cry. The room was packed full and the security detail impressed me almost more than the painting. Fifteen feet in front of the canvas stood a wall of bullet-proof glass with a do-not-cross line on the floor in front of it. An electronic eye monitored the line, and two somber Guardia Civil officers monitored the crowd, submachine guns cradled in their arms. It was only a decade after Franco's death, and only two years since *Guernica* arrived in Spain. Still, it seemed inconceivable that anyone might attack a painting about the horrors of war. Instead, the glass, the guards, the solemnity of the crowd made the mural itself seem dangerous, like a caged criminal threatening to burst forth and ravage the world.

Black, white, a palette of gray. A jumble of images: A horse with a javelin piercing its chest, head reared back and mouth open, its tongue as pointed as a dagger, hooves piercing the transparent body of a human corpse. A woman screaming, arms thrust in the air, a flaming piece of wood crushing her. The bright head of a bull turning back toward its dark body, ears and horns pointing toward the sky, tail rising up like a flame. Against its side, a wailing bare-breasted mother clutching a limp infant in her grotesque hands. A squawking bird. A head emerging from the darkness beside an outstretched arm, holding up a candle. A light bulb with the jagged glow of a child's sun. The curves of motion and the sharp angles of despair.

The second time I saw *Guernica* was very different. Nearly ten years had passed and I was living in Spain, in the northern city of Oviedo. After a visit from my New York boyfriend, I'd said good-bye to him at the Madrid airport. It had been the usual kind of good-bye, a bit teary, with declarations of love and promises about the future, but after he was gone, despair cramped at my core. I seemed to know then what it would take a long time to believe about the future of our relationship, and so, with a few hours to spare before the evening bus home to Oviedo, I took my sorrow to a place that had once made me happy.

On a winter weekday the Prado was not at all crowded. I looked in on my favorite paintings, then spent the afternoon lingering before images of the crucifixion of Christ. I felt suddenly fascinated by the way various artists rendered the same iconic moments, by the blood, the pain, the stages of fleshly mortification. There's an embarrassing, almost pornographic feel to witnessing depictions of a torn, pierced, humiliated body. As Susan Sontag writes about photographs of suffering, "There is the satisfaction of being able to look at the image without flinching. There is the pleasure of flinching." And there is also a kind of mourning that images make possible, a rehearsal of grief that tempered my sadness that day. I marveled at El Greco's long, sinewy Christ, at Goya's fleshy thighs and splayed toes. I reeled before the luminescent Christ of Velázquez, his head bowed in darkness while his torso shines, the slight shadow of abdominal muscles disappearing into a cloth wrapped low around his hips. I wanted to run my fingers along that skin, feel the solid, earthly body, offer comfort to the man on the verge of transcendence. The painting's beauty, its gruesome suffering made sublime, consoled me. Then, when there were no more Christs to feed my desire, I remembered *Guernica*.

In the Casón del Buen Retiro, the guards were no longer armed, and they stepped away from their posts from time to time, yawning. The exhibit room was nearly empty, with no more than a dozen visitors at any given moment, so I was able to stand alternately close to the glass and far enough back to see the entire composition without moving my head. In the hallway outside, a display of Picasso's early sketches showed the studies he'd made, the additions and erasures, the developing vision. I moved back and forth between these small drawings and the enormous finished product a dozen, two dozen times, caught up in the generative process of *Guernica*. Then, taking the lead of another visitor, I sat down on the floor at the back of the room, leaned against the wall, and looked until the painting seemed less like an object, static and contained behind that wall of glass, than like a recitation, a visual lexicon, a system of utterance as gorgeously complex as prayer.

In 1937, Pablo Picasso was living in Paris, monitoring from afar the Civil War in his homeland. The previous fall he'd been named Director-in-Exile of the Prado Museum, a title that made particular sense since the entire contents of the museum had been smuggled out of besieged Madrid and would eventually be stored in Switzerland. In January, representatives of Spain's Republican government visited Picasso and asked him to paint a mural to be hung in Paris that summer at the International Exposition. They were hoping for an overtly political painting, one that would join the other works in the Spanish Pavilion in denouncing the ideology and tactics of Franco's insurgency.

Although Picasso didn't consider himself a political artist, he accepted the commission and tried for months to come up with an idea. He sketched and thought and fretted, but as the spring wore on, he found himself without a plan. Then on April 26, the small Basque town of Guernica was attacked by the German air force operating at Franco's behest. It was the first full-scale aerial bombardment of a civilian population on the continent, an experiment in total warfare that would later serve as a model for the blitzkrieg and the firebombings of Hamburg and Dresden. Within days, eyewitness accounts of slaughter reached Paris, along with stark, black-and-white photographs of a completely devastated town. On May 1, more than a million people took to the streets of Paris to protest the massacre, and that afternoon, Picasso went to work.

Like many towns in Spain, Guernica had prospered during World War I by manufacturing the kinds of metal goods a war requires — bullets, machinery, even cutlery. Industrialization was fueled by the country's neutrality in the war, and the town grew into a regional center with multi-story buildings clustered around plazas and a large open-air marketplace in its center. At the start of the Spanish Civil War, about 6,000 people lived in and around Guernica.

By the fall of 1936, the Republicans held most major cities in Spain while Franco's Nationalists controlled most of the countryside, except the Basque region and neighboring Catalonia. By the spring of 1937, Nationalist forces had succeeded in cutting off most of the incoming food supply to the Basques, and people were growing desperate. April 26, a Monday, was market day in Guernica, the day when people flocked in from the countryside. Rumors of an attack had been swirling since the bombing of nearby Durango a few weeks before, and many people were afraid to go to market, but there wasn't much choice. Farmers needed whatever money they could get for livestock, whatever vegetables and flour they could find for their families.

At noon, a reconnaissance plane flew overhead as the church bells tolled a warning, but then nothing happened and people emerged from the cellars and went back to business. Some time after 4:00 PM, the first German Condor Legion plane appeared. Because Guernica was an entirely undefended town, with no means of protecting itself from assault, the plane was able to fly low and drop its bombs directly onto the market area. Fifteen minutes later — just as people were tending to the wounded, trying desperately to put out fires, reeling with disbelief — three more planes arrived, and the attack on Guernica began.

Out in the Bay of Biscay, sailors on a British ship watched as Condor Legion planes circled one by one and began their approach, a tremendous column of smoke rising over the countryside. Bound by Britain's non-intervention policy, the sailors watched for more than three hours, trying to imagine the nightmare scene on the ground.

The sky over Guernica is textured with white-gray clouds, the kind of day when anything can happen: a burst of torrential rain, a sudden blaze of sun. Outside the train station, I experience a moment of intense foreignness because a town of only 15,000 people has the immediate feel of a city. I can already see that the narrow streets are busy with traffic, that the buildings are several stories high with shops and businesses on the first floors and apartments above. The adjective that comes to mind is *European*, which I guess means compact and lively. I don't know why this surprises me.

At the tourism office a receptionist gives me a map in Euskara with Spanish translations, the heading of which is *Gernika—Bakearen Hiria*. Guernica—City of Peace. I buy a combined entry ticket to the museums, printed with a suggested itinerary: the Museum of Peace, the Udetxea Palace, the Basque Museum, and the Assembly House, where the regional government meets. The ordering of this tour makes sense, but the Museum of Peace contains an extensive exhibit on the bombing of Guernica that I'm not yet ready to visit. I quickly decide to invert the tour and get my bearings in this town before I face up to the reason I've come.

But what, I wonder, is the reason I've come?

When I turn to leave the tourism office, the receptionist calls me back. She's a young woman, perhaps in her early twenties, with a pleasant round face and the manner of a business professional. She's holding a pen poised above a notebook and looking at me as though the most important part of our conversation lies ahead. "Where are you from?" she asks.

"Excuse me?" I respond, knowing perfectly well what she's said. But it's July 2005, and in Guernica more than anywhere else I feel the weight of nationality on my shoulders. As my cheeks grow hot, the young woman repeats the question then stares at me, wide-eyed, a slight smile frozen on her face. I maneuver around the list of disclaimers in my mind and say, simply, "Los Estados Unidos." She leans forward slightly, a look of concentration on her face, and says, "I'm sorry, where?"

"Guernica is the happiest town in the world. Its affairs are run by a group of countrymen who meet beneath an oak tree and always make the fairest decisions," wrote Jean-Jacques Rousseau in the eighteenth century. A romantic claim, but it's true that in the Middle Ages the General Assemblies of Biscay, one of the oldest democratic systems in Europe, began meeting under the Tree of Guernica to make legislative decisions for the region. In the early nineteenth century, Guernica's Assembly House was built, enabling the countrymen to meet indoors, within view of the oak tree. This practice continued until the Second Carlist War ended in 1876, at which time a constitutional monarchy abolished regional sovereignty. For the next century, various forms of the Spanish government denied rights of self-rule to the Basques until, in 1979, the post-Franco administration granted limited autonomy to the region. Since then the General Assemblies of Biscay have resumed meeting in Guernica's Assembly House.

A tall, cheerful man welcomes me into the building and, after assuring me that this is a good place to begin my tour, asks where I'm from. I'm less surprised this time, but no more able to state my identity clearly. I'll be asked the same question repeatedly throughout the day — a lot of visitors come to Guernica each year, and someone must be tallying our origins. But each time I answer, trying not to mumble, the question will come back again: "I'm sorry, where?"

The Assembly House contains two main rooms, a large hall with a stained glass ceiling depicting the oak tree, and an oval meeting chamber that, with its tiers of seats and wide door looking into a grassy yard, seems like the epitome of democratic rule. Outside, a marble gazebo houses the petrified stump of a 300-year-old oak, while a descendent from that tree, planted in 1860, stands as the symbol of Basque identity. A sapling from the current tree grows just behind it, awaiting its role as successor. The 1937 attack on Guernica was carefully orchestrated to avoid the Assembly House and the oak tree. The point was to demoralize a people, to convince them that further resistance would lead to absolute devastation. But Franco didn't want the Basque soldiers in his army to rebel, and so the bridge, the market place, the bulk of the town were all destroyed, but the Assembly House and oak tree still stand.

The gray sky has broken into puffy, quick-moving clouds that let the sun through, and I remove my sweater and tie it around my waist. In the shade of a gazebo, an older British couple fan themselves, and I'm tempted to strike up a conversation with them. In the last two weeks I've spoken English only during my telephone calls home, and I miss the fluidity of extended conversation. But as I gaze out from the hillside over the town of Guernica, across the river to a forested ridge, I'm silenced by the loveliness of the scene. It feels wrong, somehow, to stand on this hillside and enjoy the beautiful day. My mind conjures up the roar of plane engines, the heart-stopping vibration of explosions, the heat and thick black smoke, the screams. I can't decide whether this imaginative exercise is ridiculous or reasonable or both, but everywhere I go in Guernica, I run through it again.

Number 19 on the map is *Picassoren "Guernica" Zeramikazko Murala*. I walk along a two-block stretch at the top of a hill, trying to locate a ceramic tile replica of Picasso's painting until, like an optical illusion, it appears right beside me, on an unassuming gray stone wall I'd already passed by. The images are so familiar—the horse, the bull, the traumatized, bare-breasted women—that at first I feel the surprised pleasure of running into an old friend. Then I cross the street to take a photo, and I'm astonished by the contrast between Picasso's stark figures and the gleaming daylight, the sound of traffic, the colorful row of apartment balconies above.

Guernica was meant to stir and haunt its viewers, to seduce and repulse them. But during its first installation at the Paris World Exposition, the painting received little attention. The Spanish Pavilion opened late, as did many of the exhibits, and it was grossly overshadowed by the more ostentatious displays of Germany and the Soviet Union. The few critics who made their way to *Guernica* were unimpressed, with one describing it as "a hodgepodge of body parts that any four-year-old could have painted."

The occasion for which *Guernica* was created was only the beginning of its life. After the Exposition closed, the painting traveled through a Britain on the verge of full-scale war, often achieving its intended effect. Picasso was already an internationally well-known artist, and his stark depiction of suffering struck a chord with many viewers. In London, Oxford, Leeds, Manchester, *Guernica* generated both outrage and amazement, drawing audiences from all walks of life. The price of admission for one show was a pair of boots, to be sent to the troops at the Spanish front, and large numbers of viewers paid with their own footwear. From England, *Guernica* embarked on a tour of major U.S. cities, then settled in New York's Museum of Modern Art where it remained, except during periods of loan, for several decades. During the Vietnam War, there was talk of relocating the painting in protest of U.S. foreign policy, but after a great deal of consultation, Picasso decided against this. In 1974, an Iranian artist walked up to the painting in MOMA and sprayed the words "Kill Lies All" across it in red paint, in protest of President Nixon's pardon of a Vietnam War lieutenant. Fortunately, because the painting had become fragile during its travels, restorers had used a protective coat of lacquer that allowed the graffiti to be wiped off.

A magnet for controversy, *Guernica* is one of the most often reproduced, most iconic paintings in the world. Postcards, photographs, artistic copies abound. Nelson Rockefeller once commissioned a tapestry version of the painting in a palette of browns and taupes, and in 1985, his estate donated the replica to the United Nations in New York. Appropriately, the tapestry now hangs outside the door to the Security Council chamber, where it serves as a powerful, constant reminder of the suffering war entails. Or at least that's the theory. On February 5, 2003, six weeks before the U.S. invasion of Iraq began, Secretary of State Colin Powell appeared before the Security Council to argue the Bush Administration's case for war. In preparation for that appearance, United Nations workers covered *Guernica* with blue curtains. The official rationale was that television crews preferred to film speeches against a solid background rather than against the chaos of eviscerated animals. But unnamed diplomatic sources reported that the U.S. government had pressured the United Nations into covering up what would have been an astonishing source of irony.

"Say it again, please? Where are you from?"

The Museum of Peace in Guernica is not anti-war. "The history of peace must not be the history of the end of conflict," the brochure declares, which catches me off guard. After wandering through the pretty town of Guernica, after learning a little bit about Basque culture and strolling through a hillside park from which I could survey the entire area that was destroyed, I've arrived at the museum bearing my indignation, my fury at what we do to one another in the name of civilization. I want to pledge my allegiance to nonviolence, sign petitions, feel that for a small part of an afternoon, I've escaped the impotence of daily life.

The first exhibit, titled "What is Peace?" has as its welcoming image an enormous, very close-up photograph of a baby suckling at a swollen breast. I stand before the display for a long time, taking in the blue eyes, round cheeks, the slight glisten of milk along the bottom lip. Everything curves—the baby's nose, chin, shoulder, eyebrow, the underside of the breast. There are no angles, no points, no straight lines to guide the eye here or there. Only shadows where flesh meets flesh. Anywhere else it would be a beautiful, arresting image, but here it makes the muscles in my back and shoulders constrict, my jaw clench. This, I think, is not what I came here for.

But of course I've forgotten where I am, in a region of Spain that has struggled violently over the last century for the right to cultural expression and self-rule. Even after the post-Franco government granted limited autonomy in 1979, the terrorist activity of ETA, the violent arm of the Basque separatists, has continued. Naturally a museum whose focal point is the bombing of the Basque heartland must be careful not to inflame its visitors too much. Anger is so strong, so physical an emotion, and peace such a difficult concept to wrap the mind around.

During the year I lived in Spain, ETA carried out a number of terrorist attacks, including a car bomb that exploded prematurely in Madrid. The bomb's target was nowhere near the site, but a woman who had been walking along the street was caught in the explosion, her legs blown off at the knees. Somehow a news cameraman got to the scene fast enough to film the woman on her back, trying to sit up. She had shoulder-length, auburn hair, wore a skirt and blouse, a light sweater. She looked as if she'd been on her way to work and then suddenly she was there on the ground, face charred, calves and feet simply gone. Ten, fifteen, twenty times a day the news stations rolled the footage of the woman struggling to sit up, her shocked eyes very white against her blackened face, two bloody stumps emerging from beneath the skirt. Ten, twenty times a day I watched, unable to turn away.

Dare I admit to the gruesome beauty of the scene? Of the woman's auburn hair, her plain cardigan sweater, the bright blue sky above the street where she lay? And to the shame of watching, over and over again, from a place of absolute safety?

A small room, dimly lit. The automatic door slides closed behind me, and I stand facing a dark glass wall. A sound recording begins of a woman's voice narrating through the day of April 26. A day that began, as these days always do, unremarkably.

A light comes on behind the glass wall, revealing the interior of a simple home, a table set for dinner, a picture on the wall. As I listen to the woman's words, her slightly British inflections, I'm conscious of a fluttering beneath my rib cage, along my neck. The horror is about to start, and I want to be ready for it, the way I'd want to be ready for a roller coaster approaching the apex of a hill, that suspended moment before inevitability takes over and you're plunged, screaming, into something you can't imagine having wanted.

When the air raid sounds, the room goes dark. Then the explosions begin, the flashes of light, and the domestic scene behind the glass reveals itself to have been an illusion, replaced now by a pile of rubble. Cement, wood pilings, crushed furniture—it's an impressive display. Yet I crave the sound of even more bombs, deafening whistles and explosions, the floor dropping from under my feet, the ceiling caving in. I want to feel fear, glimpse despair, come away from this room with the weight of experience in my center. I want to imagine my way into the unimaginable.

The next room offers news accounts, photographs, timelines, guns, grenades. The floor is made of glass rectangles looking down on a layer of rubble, a constant reminder that this building stands atop the former Guernica. I peruse the displays along with a Spanish father and son, and a young French couple who have just emerged from the bombing room. We all move slowly, reading and observing, our attention completely focused. We're traveling back and forth between reality and imagination, between the objects and stark accounts before us and the houses, the churches, the marketplace of our minds.

Eyewitness accounts of the bombing are far more gruesome than Picasso's painting. Survivors tell of blazing animals running through the streets, of people trying to crawl to safety, bones poking through their scorched skin. When the cellars filled with smoke and began to collapse under heavy bombing, hordes of people fled into the surrounding countryside where they were machine-gunned down by the low-flying planes. Words like *hell* and *apocalypse* come up over and over again in descriptions of an attack that killed over 1,600 people and wounded 800 more.

After the bombing of Guernica, fires in the city burned for three days. As soon as it was possible to enter the town, Franco's troops got to work. The munitions plant opened quickly, since Hitler was expecting payment for his favor in the form of bullets and also minerals from the rich Basque countryside. It took five years to rebuild the town fully, during which time Franco himself came often to oversee the progress. When Guernica was once again whole, the local government held a public celebration and declared Franco an adopted son of the city. There are photographs of the festivities alongside first-person accounts of how paranoid a society grows under a leadership determined to eradicate all glimmers of opposition.

Picasso, for his part, vowed never to set foot in Spain while the country remained in the hands of a fascist dictator. Nor would he allow his painting to go there. He did permit it to travel, and in the 1950s *Guernica* toured Europe and Brazil. But not Spain, never Spain, Picasso vowed, until democracy and public liberties had been restored to the country.

In 1973, Picasso died at the age of ninety-two. Franco died two years later at eighty-two. On the evening of September 10, 1981, according to a contract worked out before Picasso's death, *Guernica* arrived at the Prado Museum's Casón del Buen Retiro under heavy guard. Although there were still many people in Spain who considered Picasso a traitor to his country, the headline of *El País* the following day read, "The War Has Ended."

The main focus of the Museum of Peace is reconciliation. After the attack on Guernica, the outcry from abroad was so strong that the Nationalist propaganda machine kicked into high gear. No, no, they said, there had been no aerial bombing, Guernica was destroyed by its own inhabitants who, upon realizing that Franco's troops were closing in, demolished the town as they fled. Years later, members of the

Condor Legion admitted to their part in the attack but claimed they had only been trying to destroy the bridge into town and that the wind had carried their bombs into the marketplace. Then, on the sixtieth anniversary of the bombing of Guernica in 1997, the German ambassador attended a memorial ceremony in the town, during which he read a statement from President Herzog admitting to and apologizing for the role of the Condor Legion in the attack. This was a monumental event, considering that even post-Franco, the Spanish government and armed forces have never officially acknowledged the truth of what happened.

"What about Peace in the World Today?" the final exhibit asks. There's no idealism here, no false sense of optimism. Tiny glimmers of hope come in the form of projects like South Africa's Truth and Reconciliation Commission, in the grace exhibited by Guernica survivors in reconciling with Germany, and in the advances made in recent decades to recuperate Basque culture.

Under Franco, the identity and rich traditions of the Basque people became not only suspect but criminal. Euskara was banned from schools and heavy penalties were assigned to anyone caught speaking the language in public. This was a particular shame because Euskara is a mysterious language, unrelated to any other. Scholars believe it developed "in situ," in the geographically isolated region of northern Spain and the French Pyrenees where its dialects are still spoken today. Some linguists theorize that Euskara is a version of a prehistoric language, which might explain why words for tools like axe, knife, and hoe share a common root that means *stone*.

As a result of Franco's repression, the percentage of Basque speakers in Biscay dropped from thirty-three to less than twenty. Now an effort is underway to reverse this decline by, among other things, offering classes in Euskara to both children and adults. There are signs of progress everywhere, even though Euskara is tremendously difficult to learn as a second language. It's so difficult, in fact, that the first Basque grammar book, published by a Spanish priest in 1729, was titled *The Impossible Overcome*.

In the center of the Basque region, beneath the ceramic tile reproduction of Picasso's painting, are the words *"Guernica," Guernikara*— "Guernica" for Guernica. This slogan is a reminder that the original painting will never travel north to the region that inspired it. After a dozen years in the Casón del Buen Retiro, the fragile canvas was relocated for the final time to Madrid's Reina Sofía Museum, where it hangs in the company of other masterpieces of the twentieth century. No longer enclosed in glass, the painting seems more contemporary now, as if it has breath, a heartbeat, a relevant place in the world.

"Guernica," Guernikara. These words rattle around in my brain throughout the day, as I sip a glass of wine on a hotel terrace then decipher the map and understand that I'm looking out on the former market square. Or as I walk down a street named for Picasso and realize that the artist himself may never have set foot in this town. Nothing in the painting corresponds to the specifics of this place, to the Oka River or the oak tree or the hillside above the Assembly House where the Park of the Peoples of Europe now sprawls. The painting is not about the tortured body of this town. It's not about physical reality at all but about the imaginative space that awareness of atrocity fills.

Why have I come to Guernica today? Because the idea of it has occupied a corner of my imagination since I first encountered the painting many years ago. Because I wanted to know more about the attack, to see the contours of the scarred landscape and face up to what Susan Sontag calls, in *Regarding the Pain of Others*, "the existence of the incorrigible." Because I'm an American who cannot justify aerial assaults on Baghdad and Fallujah and Mosul by remembering images of the World Trade Center burning and falling. Because I don't know what to do with the tremendous sense of complicity I carry around with me, and so I've brought it here, to "Guernica—City of Peace," hoping for some kind of catharsis.

Which, of course, does not come. What happens instead is that I leave the Museum of Peace feeling both stirred up and exhausted, then walk beneath a sky that has darkened once again, to the train station at the edge of town. I sit down on a bench where, moments later, a heavy-set man sits down beside me, chanting in a sorrowful voice about today's date, his father's birthday, the likelihood of rain. When the train arrives, we both board the second of two cars. I've been looking forward to the ride, to the preternaturally green landscape and the possibility of hearing Euskara spoken more frequently by the passengers out here than in the city of Bilbao. Instead, what I hear is the intermittent bellowing of the man at the back of the car, and I'm reminded of how impossible it is to fully imagine ourselves into other perspectives. I'm not afraid of the man, but his unsettling voice reminds me that fear is always just a heartbeat away.

The other passengers may well be more disturbed than I am. It's 6:30 PM. Most of these people have turned on the television at some point today, used the Internet, seen the images out of London, where four bombs went off this morning, three of them on trains. It's been sixteen months since a similar terrorist attack on the Madrid subway, and this man's bellowing has got to be striking a nerve. I won't understand this for another hour, until I arrive back in Bilbao, walk to a grocery store for dinner supplies, then stroll to my hotel and spread a picnic on the bed. Until I aim the remote control in the direction of the television and lift a grape toward my mouth, taking in its hard roundness, the slight give of the skin before it snaps.

Throughout his life, Picasso was barraged by questions about the meaning of *Guernica*. What does the horse signify? Is the bull a symbol of Spain? And what about the sun that is also a light bulb, what does that say about the future of the country? Tell us in words, people seemed to demand, what you've already said in images. But some things cannot be translated, Picasso insisted. "These are animals, massacred animals. That's all as far as I'm concerned."

Tomorrow, my last full day in Bilbao, I'll visit the Museum of Fine Arts. "Paris and the Surrealists" is the traveling exhibit, and I'll seek out the most grotesque images of all, the exquisite corpses, with their mismatched heads, torsos, and legs. I'll take solace in these drawings, in the abject portrayals of bodies and desires. Unmediated reality will not appeal to me at all tomorrow, but gruesome beauty, the patterns and disjunctions of the artistic mind, will. In the meantime, tonight, I watch television for far too long, hypnotized by the images: a bloody-faced young man sitting on the ground, a woman walking with a white paper mask held to her skin, the charred skeleton of a double-decker bus. I flip back and forth among the stations until there's nothing new anywhere, until the satisfaction of not flinching and the pleasure of flinching have cancelled each other out. Then I switch to the Basque channel and let Euskara fill the room, comforting me with its impossible sounds and rhythms, relieving me for the moment of trying to understand.

Part Three. After Spain

In Praise of Envy

A fter he leaves for work in the morning, I pour some tea, wave a piece of string in front of the kitten's face, go upstairs to shower but, oh, there's that quotation I want to check, so it's back downstairs, through the living room, to the door of his office. Inside it's dark, cool, messy. Papers are scattered on the desk, along with stacks of index cards and a perpetually opened dictionary. I find the book I have in mind, *Absalom, Absalom!*, take it off the shelf, and sit down in his chair to see what I can see from here.

Not much. Everything appears the same as it did yesterday, so I slide open the first drawer. Just looking for a pen, anyway. If he walked in right now — even though he's halfway to the university where his first class starts in an hour — he'd see me sitting here, innocently enough, looking for a pen with which to write down the quotation I'm checking.

That's Envy talking, rationalizing. That's Envy sidling up like a best friend, putting her arm around my shoulder. "You and me, baby. We're in this together. Now let's see what's in that next drawer down."

Nothing of interest. And nothing in the next or the next. But then, at the back of the bottom drawer, under some airmail letters from me, I discover an expired datebook. It's small, thin, with a mottled red cover and spiral binding, the edges of its pages slightly worn. Its calendar follows the academic year, August to August, and since we're now into September, I might be in luck.

Envy's breath is sweet and warm on my neck. "You've crossed a line already by finding the thing, right? There's no point in stopping now."

At the rear of the book is a list of phone numbers. The two that are mine include the apartment in nearby Rosendale, where I lived until last summer, and the flat I shared in Oviedo, Spain, for most of the past year. Looking at these numbers, I feel momentarily confused, unsure where I live now or how one might reach me. I scan the list, but all the names are familiar, so I flip the pages one at a time, working backward through the weeks and months, orienting myself. In August, there's just a faculty meeting and his brother's birthday. In July, a dental appointment, car repair, grocery list. Nothing incriminating. This is as I expect since if he's telling the truth, he hasn't seen her for months. Then again, even if he's not telling the truth, he hasn't seen much of her with me around.

Day by day I proceed, through the upheaval of June (including a notation on the 6th: *pick M. up at airport, 3:15*), through May's burst of fragrant green, April's prankster snow. Through the chill rains of March to late February. And then, on Friday the 20th, Envy leaps up, long arms punching the air above her head: "A-ha!" *8 pm Kelly Connaugh*. I'm surprised by how lightly the letters skim the page, how tentatively his hand must have held the pen as he scheduled their first date.

It takes a moment for me to start breathing again. And then, with Envy cheering me on, what could be easier? An unusual last name, a telephone book, a county map. From February 20th to the street where she lives, fifteen miles away, takes no time at all.

Historically, Envy has gotten a bad rap. Also known as coveting, Envy provokes warnings throughout the Bible, from the Ten Commandments to Ecclesiasticus 30:24, "Envy and wrath shorten the life." Petrarch ranks Envy among the five great enemies of peace (the others being avarice, ambition, anger, and pride), and Francis Bacon calls it "the vilest affection, and the most depraved." Samuel Johnson — to whom Envy was no stranger — goes even further: "Envy is mere unmixed and genuine evil; it pursues a hateful end by despicable means and desires not so much its own happiness as another's misery."

But the Envy I know isn't as bad as all that. The Envy I know is wry and witty, a good companion. She's intrepid, tenacious, encouraging. Her favorite line, spoken in a sultry, bourbon-and-cigarette voice, is: "Who *says* you can't?" Envy has personality, pluck. There's a spark about her that's hard to resist.

Envy is often confused with her second cousin, Jealousy. He comes around when a rival threatens to take something — or someone —

away from you, and he's prone to violence, to exacting revenge. Envy, on the other hand, is less concerned with a beloved object or person than with the rival herself. Envy wants to know how you stack up against the competition, what she has that you don't. As contemporary philosopher Aaron Ben-Ze'ev so astutely observes, Envy is motivated by a "more equal distribution of fortunes" and is "based upon firmer moral foundations than jealousy."

Here's the difference: Let's say a man and a woman have been in a relationship for a couple of years when the woman accepts a teaching position abroad. It's a good position but means an academic year away, and the pair stay in close touch while she's gone. When the man visits her during winter break, they agree that the time apart has been critical, decisive. They vow not to be separated like this again. As soon as she returns in June, they'll begin to plan their wedding.

But then a few weeks after the man goes back to New York State, he takes up with another woman, someone who's available every day of the week, whom he can call without calculating time differences. And when the first woman returns, he tells her about the affair and apologizes, explaining that he's a weak man, that he needs companionship, but that with his true love back home where she belongs, everything will return to the way it used to be.

You might expect the first woman to feel (among other things — enraged, shattered) *jealous* of the second, who appropriated her beloved for a time. And you might expect the second woman to feel *envious* of the first because maybe she really liked the guy and now, in spite of all of her pithy comments and cool passion, the first woman's back in town and he hasn't so much as called to say good-bye. That's one way for emotions to go.

But there's another way, the way it actually happened. Of course Jealousy came to stay for a while, holding up photographs of how happy we used to be and emphasizing the guy's positive characteristics. That smile, that intelligence, that sense of humor. It was Jealousy who convinced me to move into the run-down farmhouse, Jealousy who insisted that I wouldn't lose him without a fight, that if the tramp so much as called while I lived in this house, she'd be sorry. But a few months later, when it became clear that the guy wasn't leaving me for anyone (and when I started to wonder if I'd leave him instead), Jealousy quietly slipped away. In his place came Envy, with her high heels and jangling bracelets and a bright red suitcase she heaved onto my bed. The suitcase was filled with glossy photographs of beautiful, smart, talented women, women who as girls had gathered together in the hallway between classes, running their hands through each other's silky hair, sharing lip gloss. Envy brings with her a longing that stretches back through the years, through all the moments of vulnerability and exhilaration. She's savvier than Jealousy and more seductive. She arouses and, in so doing, begins to console.

In Western literature, Envy has been personified primarily as a man. In the medieval allegory, *Piers Plowman*, Envy is both male and pale, "like a leek that has lain too long in the sun." He behaves badly, telling malicious lies about the people he scorns until first doctors with leeches and then Jesus Christ himself intervene. In Spenser's "The Faerie Queen," Envy is also male, a backbiter who spews poison. He rides on the fifth beast that draws Vanity's coach, chewing,

> Betweene his cankered teeth a venomous tode,
> That all the poison ran about his chaw;
> But inwardly he chawed his owne maw
> At neighbours wealth, that made him ever sad;
> For death it was, when any good he saw,
> And wept, that cause of weeping none he had,
> But when he heard of harme, he wexed wondrous glad.

This Envy is a vile creature, torn apart by success in any form. My Envy shudders as she reads about him, her coral fingernails tapping on the desk. "That guy," she declares, "is a real head case."

In a present-day allegory, the movie *Seven*, Envy is again depicted as male, a serial killer who chooses his victims according to the seven deadly sins. Because the killer envies the detective who pursues him, he cuts off the head of the detective's wife and delivers it to her husband in a box. But here's the interesting part: during the filming of *Seven*, Gwyneth Paltrow, who played the detective's wife, began a relationship with her on-screen husband, Brad Pitt, that landed them on the cover of every celebrity magazine on the newsstand. They became America's most perfect couple, Hollywood's reigning queen and king, with every step of their romance documented in *People*. Their engagement was worth any number of headlines, and their break-up soon after was worth even more. Why? Envy, of course.

In contemporary American culture we rely on Envy to a greater extent than at any other point in history. Advertisements — including the covers of magazines — use her to create desire, to sell products and ideas to those of us who covet the blissful lives and flawless expressions of the people they feature. Gwyneth Paltrow, for example, is someone I know far too much about. She's tall and talented, blond and beautiful, very thin and very wealthy. Gwyneth is a fashion icon. Gwyneth does yoga every day. Gwyneth loves Victorian novels. Gwyneth won the Oscar for best actress, then went to bed for a week because she felt so overwhelmed. Reading about her brilliance, reaching for the next magazine that celebrates her "willowy, angelic form," I'll confess to turning pale as a leek.

But that doesn't mean I wish her ill. It doesn't make me want to see her head in a box. When Gwyneth's romance with Brad ended so publicly, did I feel even the slightest twinge of satisfaction, the least inclination to revel in another's misery? Not for a moment. The Envy I know is female, for one thing. She doesn't feed on venomous toads. She compares and evaluates, yes, but she also imagines and admires. She's prone to sarcasm and a bit of crankiness, but she's not evil. She doesn't gloat. She isn't a sin so much as a way of life.

Once when I press him (it's late, I've worn him down), he tells me she's an artist. But of course there's no money in that, so she's thinking of going to graduate school for psychology. He shakes his head and says she could definitely use some training in psychology, and I bite the inside of my cheek to keep from saying what seems obvious: "So could you."

He's trying to convince me she isn't someone to be envied. And I want to be convinced, so I pay attention to the tiny sparks of information that escape his mouth. She grew up in Woodstock, New York, a town known for its art and music scenes. She's had a rough couple of years and is now staying with her parents until she makes a decision about school or saves some money. I want to scoff, "She's twenty-seven years old and lives with her parents?" but Envy reminds me I'm older than that — and look where I live.

Envy, you see, plays fair.

On the telephone, her voice is surprisingly strong and clear. It says, "Hi, this is Kelly. I'm not in right now . . ." with no hint of the fragility he describes. I want to ask him about the discrepancy, but I know he'll just square his jaw and sigh with exasperation. He wants to please, please, please forget about her, but I want the opposite. I want to know what she looks like. Where she works. What kind of life she leads. I think it's unfair of him to withhold that information, on top of everything else. Finally, after I've worn him down some more, he offers the tiniest morsel: "She looks vaguely like my sister, OK?"

Envy shrieks and claps both hands over her mouth. His sister, of course, is drop-dead, eat-your-heart-out, Gwyneth-Paltrow gorgeous.

To the east of Route 209, the Shawangunk Ridge slopes toward flat-lands; to the north and west, the blue-green Catskills rise. This is beautiful country, inspiring country, a landscape of gentle drama. I imagine growing up in a village at the base of these mountains, a place where creativity floats on the fresh, fresh air. It's clear she's had all the advantages.

I follow 209 to 28 West to a county road that, if I stayed on it for a couple of miles, would lead me to the center of Woodstock, past the village green lined with shops and galleries. Instead, I turn into what looks like a housing development. I'm hoping for raised ranches, but no, not even close. These houses don't replicate each other, don't follow some lazy builder's plan. They're set back from the street by idyllic lawns, mature oak and birch trees in the front yards. Number twenty-nine is a white colonial with black shutters and a red door. I slow down, arms trembling, then turn around in a cul-de-sac and pass by again.

The yard is nicely kept, the driveway empty. The front and back living room windows line up so I can see clear through the house to the woods out back. That bay window over to the left must be the dining room, where the happy family gathers at meal times. The smaller window upstairs looks like the bathroom, where she showers, shaves her long legs, pulls stray hairs from her eyebrows with a slip-pery tweezer. On either side of the bathroom are bedrooms, one of them probably hers.

Alongside the house next door, an elderly man stands clipping a juniper bush. He turns, watches my car, raises the tip of his shears in the air as he nods. I smile and wave back. For all he knows, I belong here. For all he knows I live a few streets away, in this very neighborhood which is not anything, not even remotely anything, like the neighborhoods where I have lived.

And then it's over. A right, a left, and I'm back out on the highway, heading home. I feel soothed, calmer than I have in weeks. The late morning sun warms my skin, the air carries a scent of pine and that first, sweet hint of decay. I ease into the curves and press down on the straightaways, knowing already that each trip from now on will be the same: furtive, essential. On the drive there I'll feel nervous and ashamed, and on the way back I'll breathe deeply, enjoying the sense of release. With the radio blasting, Envy will keep time on the dashboard, rocking and swaying, the two of us singing to the skies.

Herodotus got it right. Or at least more right than the others. "Envy is natural to man from the beginning," he said. "How much better a thing it is to be envied than to be pitied." With Pity, the great patronizer, I would not want to spend five minutes. But even now, all these years later, when Envy shows up, poking at me until I'm up off the couch and casting about for something productive to do, it's a good day.

Envy's an optimist. As Faulkner explains in *Absalom, Absalom!*, "you only envy whom you believe to be, but for accident, in no way superior to yourself: and what you believe, granted a little better luck than you have had heretofore, you will someday possess . . ." Perhaps that's why I enjoy Envy's company. She's by my side, preaching patience. She's a critic, too, happy to point out my deficiencies. But in the process, she assures me I'm just as deserving, if not more so, than the people who preoccupy me.

Years after I've taken the kitten and moved away from the old farmhouse, I find myself sharing the foyer of a Vermont diner with Gwyneth Paltrow. I'm coming in, she's going out, and in that brief instant Envy creates a list: no make-up, uncombed hair, shoulder blades so sharp they make me cringe. I turn and watch through the window as Gwyneth gets into her car, lights a cigarette. "What does she have that you don't—besides that Audi 5000 convertible?" Envy asks, and it works. I don't begrudge Gwyneth the car, the lifestyle, the paychecks, and I don't feel bad about myself by comparison.

Before the Audi's out of the parking lot, Envy springs open her suitcase and starts to rummage through the films, the men, the photos, the comments from directors and designers about Gwyneth's grace and charm. "It's just luck and timing, all of it," she insists. Then she squares her shoulders and adds, "But my hell is she beautiful. Did you see her? A little skinny, sure, but so what? That one's as close to perfect as they come."

Envy, you see, *loves* to admire. That's what so many men have missed, the thinkers and writers who caution against her company. When Goethe wrote, "Hatred is active, and envy passive dislike; there is but one step from envy to hate," he was forgetting the pleasure, the gratification, the way Envy holds up a distorted mirror that takes you outside yourself. Envy yokes together opposing emotions: hope and disillusion, confidence and humility, love and regret—but she doesn't let you sit around passively observing these emotions. Envy engages the imagination, motivates, capacitates. Sometimes, I would argue, there is but one step from Envy to Love.

For example: It wasn't just two or three times that I drove thirty miles, round trip, to pass the house of a woman I'd never met. I spent an entire fall traveling this way. In the middle of a Friday afternoon, I'd be sitting in front of my computer, candles burning in the sunshine behind me, and Envy would start to pace, heels clicking, skirt rustling. I'd get up for a drink of water, step out onto the front porch, where the breeze was as warm and fragrant as redemption, then go back inside and try to concentrate. But Envy's desire won out every time.

Most days I remembered to blow out the candles, but sometimes they were still burning when I got back, the kitten blinking and yawning in a windowsill nearby. Some days the computer was on, too, as if I'd gotten bad news and gone running from the house, leaving Miles Davis on continuous play. Some days I stalled and thought about not doing it, watching the clock until there was barely enough time left, until I had to drive much faster than the speed limit in order to get there and home again before he returned from work. On those days it was like a game, waiting until the last moment and then, as if overtaken by madness, speeding north to the edge of the Catskills, down the familiar street, past the house where sometimes there were cars, sometimes a middle-aged man or woman walking toward the mailbox, but never her.

If I'd been determined, I could have seen her. I could have expanded my drives into the weekends or gone at night to figure out which car was hers, then waited along the county road in the early morning and followed her to work. That, and more, is what Jealousy would have urged me to do. But Envy was less interested in seeing the actual woman than in tending to the fantasies I developed about her during the drives. In one recurring scenario, I imagined having a terrible accident on the highway near her home, just as she was returning from work. As the first person on the scene, she would come to me, bending into my car, her long blond hair falling across my chest. She would appear willowy, angelic, with eyes the color of a midday sea. And oh, how she would smell. Like a hint of French perfume, like a church when you first walk in, like something sacred. She would take my hand and ask how much it hurt, then tell me not to worry, everything would be OK. And I would know, and she would not, that I was who I was — and she was the woman I wanted to be.

I drove and drove that autumn because I sought the only real consolation I could imagine: that Envy's presence would be fully justified. I wanted to surrender to my rival, to be humbled by her, to feel myself pale in every conceivable way beside her. Because only then, only when I knew how otherworldly she was, how luminous and compelling, could I admit that he'd been justified in turning to her. Only then could I forgive him.

Always when I returned from these trips, I felt better. And almost always I made it back before he did. The one time I didn't, when I pulled into the driveway behind his car and he held open the kitchen door, calling, "Where were you — I was worried," I felt chagrined and satisfied all at once. I considered making up a story but instead shrugged and said, in the most gracious tone I could manage, "Out for a drive." And to his credit, he didn't ask, didn't demand, didn't press me on the music or the candles. He just stepped aside, trying as hard as he could — though the effort was doomed — to accommodate the dolled-up woman, snapping her gum, sauntering through the door behind me.

Fluency

hen I'm tired, weary from a day spent teaching or writing, or perhaps from a general period when too many things are going on at once, I develop an embarrassing speech tic. Words come out of my mouth unpredictably, sometimes in direct opposition to what I mean to say — *summer* instead of *winter*, *night* in place of *day* — and sometimes with only a tangential relationship to my thoughts. After a satisfying meal, arms folded across my stomach and eyelids drooping, I might sigh, "That was terrific. Now I'm really *hungry*." I mean *sleepy*, of course, and if I'm with good friends, I won't even bother correcting myself. I'll just wave my hand in the air and they'll nod, translating. But if my companions aren't close to me, aren't people who know about this tic and accept it the way they accept so many of my idiosyncrasies, there's a terrible pause while everyone registers the nonsense I've just spoken. *Is she OK?* I can see them thinking. *Did she drink too much? Does she have a brain tumor?*

I used to wonder about the last question myself, since a medical condition seemed the only way to account for things going so wrong in the nanosecond between thinking of an idea and hearing my own words. I wondered, too, if there were a psychological explanation for the problem, if these language errors were pieces of dream-life bursting into my waking existence. Once in particular that seemed to be the case, when I was in my mid-twenties, active, and a vegetarian, yet a cholesterol test came back astonishingly high. Upon receiving the results I complained dramatically to my boyfriend, intending to say, "I feel like I have mayonnaise *coursing* through my *veins*." But it was a Friday afternoon, the end of a particularly long week, and what came out instead was: "I feel like I have mayonnaise *cursing* through my *veil*."

I gasped when I heard the words then gave a weak laugh, but my boyfriend wasn't amused. "Now there's a Freudian slip," he scowled. It was true that he'd been bringing up the topic of marriage lately and that the prospect interested him much more than it did me. He took my mistake to mean something negative about my emotions, our relationship, the future, and although I denied it, I secretly thought he was right.

Now, years later, my language mix-ups have happened so frequently and with such awkward and amusing results that I've stopped trying to interpret them. I no longer worry about what causes the problem. Maybe a synapse misfires or my blood sugar falls too low, or maybe it's a birth defect, a tiny flaw in the gene that controls speech. All I'm certain of is that this tic has appeared so regularly for so long that it can't come from a brain tumor. Clearly it's connected to fatigue, but beyond that I've given up trying to understand my verbal mistakes. Winter/summer, hungry/sleepy, veins/veil—close enough, I say.

I realize this is a strange, almost blasphemous, attitude for a writer to have. A writer should care deeply about the precision of language, about getting things exactly right. And most of the time I do. But I'm also deeply suspicious of language, which has never seemed fully on my side. In college I was stunned silent in more than one creative writing class by the way some students talked about the words on the page. They seemed to own the language in which they wrote, to believe it would represent their ideas accurately. I remember one classmate in particular, a woman with pale blond hair and ethereal skin, speaking intensely about the beauty and complexity of words. There was something like rapture in her voice as she declared that she *loved* language, its sounds and rhythms, its double and triple entendres, its etymology.

Or was it entomology? There it is again, that trickster figure, that shape-shifting foe. The history of words/the study of insects . . . language confounds me at least as often as it delights. With unnerving frequency a word forms at the back of my throat, rolls like a marble along my tongue, solid and weighty, and when my lips push it out into the world, I expect it to arc and land with an impressive thump.

Instead, no sooner does it leave my body than it pauses, begins to flutter, and takes to the sky.

There's some small comfort in knowing I'm not alone in these struggles, that language plays tricks on other people as well, sometimes leaving controversies in its wake.

In 1999, an aide to the mayor of Washington, D.C., was having a budget meeting with two colleagues. During the course of the discussion the aide, David Howard, mentioned a particular fund that was low and said he would have to be "niggardly" with it. Howard is white, and the colleagues—one black and the other white—were horrified by what they heard. In fact, the word *niggardly* comes from a Scandinavian root that means stingy or ungenerous and has no linguistic or historical relationship to the Latin word *niger*, which means black. Even so, the miscommunication resulted in Howard offering his resignation to Anthony Williams, D.C.'s newly elected black mayor.

When I read about the situation in the newspaper, I gasped aloud, mortified for everyone involved. That's language in a nutshell, I thought. It takes on a life of its own, becoming something you never meant it to be, something over which you have no control.

After Williams accepted Howard's resignation, the furor really began. Julian Bond, former Chairman of the NAACP, criticized the mayor's decision, saying, "You hate to think you have to censor your language to meet other people's lack of understanding." Rush Limbaugh jumped into the fray, lamenting that "some poor overeducated slob" had lost his job over a Swedish word. A *Wall Street Journal* letter-writer from Georgia said the situation reminded him of his childhood in the Rust Belt, where "the fastest way to get beat up was usin' big words. A large vocabulary can be a liability when dealing with the ignorant."

For me, though, the issue had less to do with ignorance than with the maddening proximity words can have to one another. As it happened, I knew the meaning of the word *niggardly* before I read the article. Maybe I'd discovered it long ago in a nineteenth-century novel and been startled by its proximity to taboo. Probably I'd looked it up in the dictionary, said it aloud a couple of times to test the *d* sound, skeptical that a legitimate word could have such strong echoes. But I don't believe I've ever used the word, in conversation or on paper, because of the way it sounds. And even knowing the meaning of the word, I think I, too, would have been taken aback to hear David Howard use it.

Howard seemed to understand why. In a public apology (after which Mayor Williams re-hired him), Howard said, "It's an arcane word that's unfamiliar to a lot of people. You have to be able to see things from the other person's shoes, and I did not do that." He also explained that he'd learned the word while studying for his SAT's in high school. He didn't own it, he seemed to be saying—that word, the language he'd used in speaking, didn't reflect who he was.

But how can we ever be sure that language reflects who we are? And more to the point, who are we apart from language? That's a question I've struggled with mightily, in part because, unlike David Howard, for most of my life I haven't had to worry about whether people will understand the words I use. Quite the opposite, in fact. In my studies and my profession, I've often felt so far behind in the language department it seemed I might never catch up.

Shortly after finishing my undergraduate degree in English, I took the GRE exams for graduate school without studying beforehand. It didn't occur to me that anyone studied for this kind of test, which I thought measured what you knew—really knew. Studying seemed a form of cheating. Even after receiving my mortifyingly low scores, it didn't occur to me to study and retake the test. Instead, I revised my perception of myself from someone who had excelled in college to someone who had clearly learned *nothing* in the last four years. My lack of knowledge was encapsulated in all the exam words I didn't know. Most had looked familiar, sounded familiar, I'd been sure I'd seen them in stories and essays. But without a context, in a question like "urbane is to gaucherie as _____ is to _____," I was completely at a loss.

A couple years later, and despite my low GRE scores, I was accepted into a Master's program in English Literature at a nearby state university, where I was also invited to teach Freshman Composition. As I prepared to begin the program, I felt like the ash-girl on her way to the ball. My vocabulary seemed paltry, threadbare. People would see right through it, I feared, and understand that admitting me had been a mistake. I was working then as a part-time writing tutor at a local community college, and during the summer before I began the graduate program, the math tutor and I would sometimes go whole days without seeing students. While he read science fiction novels, I used that time to study words. The community college library was stocked with vocabulary-building guides, and I borrowed an armful. I typed out lists, made flash cards, enlisted the math tutor to quiz me through the As — abate, accede, acerbic, adjudicate, antebellum — and then on to other letters. He'd flash *belie* and I'd wrinkle my brow, unsure whether it meant "to lie about" or "not to lie about." He'd flash *celerity, dichotomy, efface, foment,* and sometimes I'd get them all right, but when we reviewed these same words a few days later, it was as if I'd pressed my mind's erase button. I felt like a charlatan, about to begin a teaching career in English without really knowing the language.

I tried mnemonic devices, I tried studying roots, prefixes, and suffixes, but none of it helped. The problem wasn't with my memorization skills, it was with my attitude toward this new, intimidating vocabulary. I'd never heard these words spoken in my daily life, not at home or among friends, and like the letter-writer from Georgia, I'd grown up with a skepticism toward people whose way of talking made others feel stupid. So I couldn't use my new words, and without using them I didn't feel they belonged to me. They didn't reflect who I was.

When the fall semester began I quickly got my bearings in graduate school. I relaxed around the students who seemed on par with me in their knowledge and speech, and I stayed fairly quiet while observing the few who intimidated me. Then one night after a raucous department party, a handsome guy with a frighteningly large vocabulary asked me for a ride home. During the classes we shared, I kept a list of the unfamiliar words he used and looked them up when I got home, marveling each time at how precise they were, how perfectly suited to the idea he'd expressed. What would it feel like, I wondered, to trust all those words, to be confident in your ability to say exactly what you meant, every time?

As we walked to my car after the party, he seemed to be flirting. He tried to convince me to take up a musical instrument, saying that the guitar was easy and he could give me lessons. A full moon shone above and the faintest possibility of a crush fluttered around in my ribs. "Trust me," I responded, laughing, "I'm completely disinterested in playing the guitar."

Right then, my nightmare came true. He winced as if in pain and stopped walking. "Oh man," he said. "It drives me crazy when people misuse that word. *Dis*interested means impartial, objective. As in, a judge should be a disinterested party. You mean *un*interested."

The wind went out of me and the hair on my arms stood up. He'd seen through me in exactly the way I'd feared, and my first impulse was to be thankful that no one else had heard this exchange. My second impulse was to call this guy a pompous ass, because how rude do you have to be to lecture someone you barely know? And yet I couldn't argue with what he'd said. I had misused the word, not because I'd been drinking but because I didn't know the difference, and I wanted to know the difference. I wanted to learn, and here was someone who apparently couldn't help but teach.

"OK. I am completely *un*interested in playing the guitar," I said. "And also in driving you home."

He threw his head back, laughing, and grasped my upper arm with his long fingers. "Too late," he said, which was true.

The romance that began that night helped change my attitude toward language. I became less suspicious of the kind of vocabulary I wanted to develop and more willing to try out new words. I also noticed that when we were alone or with a group of close friends, or when we went to visit his parents, the intimidating guy was much more plain-spoken than he was in class. At first I thought this meant his elevated language was a way of pretending to be someone he really wasn't. But later I understood that we all shift languages depending on the circumstance, even those of us who think our vocabularies are too small for that. Knowing this made me hopeful that I, too, could learn to speak in a greater range of voices, becoming comfortable with a new kind of fluency.

As a test of this possibility, just as I completed my Master's degree I was offered a year-long teaching position at a university in Spain. Whereas my difficulties with the English language continued to trouble me, my almost complete lack of Spanish vocabulary didn't give me a moment's hesitation. In high school and college I'd studied foreign languages—some Spanish and French, a little bit of German, and gotten high grades in those courses, and I believed I had a knack for foreign language. In fact, what I have a knack for is reading. I can decipher words on the page and come away with the gist—if not the nuances—of meaning. But as I learned shortly after moving to Spain, when it comes to speaking in another language, my brain quickly grows tired and my verbal tic comes out in all its glory.

In Spain, my housemate was a generous, open-minded woman whose patience I constantly tried. Over and over she explained the difference between "la bañera" and "el bañador," and over and over, I confused the two. "Have you seen my bathtub?" I'd ask, and Lola would shake her head, roll her eyes. "I hung your bathtub in the swim-suit," she'd reply, and only later, while walking to the university pool and replaying the conversation in my head, would I understand and laugh out loud.

I had an especially hard time with words that sounded alike to me but not to Spanish people. A general rule in Spanish is that nouns ending in *o* (niño, chico) are masculine, while those ending in *a* (niña, chica) are feminine. But sometimes a word's final letter changes its meaning entirely. *Moros*, for example, are Moors, while *moras* are blackberries, a difference I discovered after telling Lola that I liked to bake scones with fresh North Africans in them. "No, you don't," she responded, smiling, and I squared my shoulders, placed my hands on my hips. For once I was sure I was right.

After we'd consulted a dictionary and sorted out the problem, I vented my frustration. "It's just one letter," I moaned. "You could have figured it out. You know I sometimes confuse *o* and *a* at the end of a word."

"That's not how we think in Spanish," Lola explained. "They're two entirely different words, unconnected. For all I knew, you could have been confusing the first letters."

"But I never confuse first letters!" I protested, and Lola burst out laughing, slipping an arm around my shoulder. "You," she said, "con-fuse *every*thing."

Of course it was true. In Spanish as in English my relationship with language was haphazard at best. I read and studied and memorized, but when I started to speak it was anybody's guess whether I'd make sense. And yet, curiously, my difficulties with Spanish never felt like the kind of moral failing that my struggles with English seemed to be. In English it was as if I'd started out behind, as if there were a body of knowledge and experience that others had effortlessly taken in but that, for reasons I didn't understand and felt ashamed of, I had failed to absorb. In Spanish, although I often felt frustrated, my attitude toward myself remained compassionate. As the year progressed, I felt I was making friends with the language, gathering words around me in a festive way. One of my favorite phrases was, *¿Qué quiere decir?* "What does that mean?" It was a question I rarely asked aloud in English, but in Spanish I repeated it like a blissfully naïve child.

Language is power. Everyone knows that, most of us from a personal experience in which words saved us or in which we felt inferior to someone else who spoke well. And some of us are so bothered by not having the power of language that we go to great lengths to acquire it.

Once, long before I moved to Spain, I was having a drink with a friend when a couple of guys approached us at the bar. One was from the Dominican Republic and the other was American, and the second guy asked if either of us spoke Spanish. "She does," my friend said, although it wasn't true, and the American guy urged me toward his buddy. "Here, talk to him in his own language," he said.

"I don't really speak Spanish," I explained, and the Dominican guy said, "That's OK," then switched to Spanish. I asked questions like *¿Cómo estás?* and *¿Dónde trabajas?*—How are you? Where do you work?—but I had trouble understanding his responses because I had no ear for the language, for the way it sounds in real life as opposed to in a classroom. After a few moments, he switched back to English. "You speak so good," he said. "You speak the right way. You been to college, right?"

I gave a self-deprecating response, but he waved it away. "No, you speak real good," he repeated. "I never been to college. You speak better than me." I suspected he was flirting, or even making fun of me, but soon I realized that what he was saying was deferential. The way Spanish sounded on my lips, the way I pronounced every letter because I didn't know how not to, gained me respect in his eyes. I was sorry that my pronunciation intimidated him, especially since I'd used every Spanish word I remembered in our short exchange. At the same time, it felt fantastic to be seen as if I'd accomplished something in my life, as if going to college and studying foreign languages meant something in and of itself.

Later, there were many reasons why I decided to spend some of my time in Spain making applications to PhD programs back in the United States. Among the smallest, perhaps, was the memory of that day in the bar and how powerful I'd felt when a perfect stranger offered respect for the way I spoke. I didn't deserve that respect, but I nonetheless got it into my head that, like the scarecrow in *The Wizard of Oz*, only a degree stood between me and absolute confidence in my way with words.

As concerned as I'd been about my language skills the first time I entered graduate school, I began a PhD program nearly paralyzed by anxiety. The deficient vocabulary I brought with me felt like a dark secret I constantly tried to hide, like alcoholism or sexual perversion. During the next few years, the English language sometimes felt more foreign to me than Spanish ever had. Words like *hegemony*, *reification*, *cooption*, and *praxis* echoed off the classroom walls, and terms like *performativity* made me doubt even the words I did know. I made my way, slowly and painfully, through articles and books whose sentences looped back on each other, tying themselves into bows, the faint outline of a middle finger seeming to rise from their pages. I wasn't alone in feeling demoralized by this, and it helped to commiserate with classmates. But it still seemed that I, more than everyone else, was trying to build a flimsy house on a very shaky foundation.

Once during this second phase of graduate school, I was about to drive several friends to a pub when I noticed a pool of greenish liquid under the front end of my car. "Uh-oh," I said, popping the hood and crossing my fingers that the leak came from a bad hose, but the radiator was hemorrhaging antifreeze. I wondered aloud whether I could keep enough fluid in it to drive to a garage instead of calling a tow truck, and suddenly, out of what seemed like the blue, my friend Seth asked, "Did you grow up working class?"

"Why?" I responded, my cheeks aflame. I quickly scrolled back through what had just happened: I'd cursed upon realizing where the leak was coming from, and I'd groaned aloud about how much a new radiator would cost. But we were all students—none of us had extra money. And Seth himself cursed like a sailor, and burped and farted without apology. How could he tell?

"That's what I love about working-class people," he said. "When there's a problem with your car, you just open the hood and figure out what it is." There was a tone of admiration in his voice, like he wanted to pat me on the back and buy me a shot of whiskey, and I struggled with how to respond. On the one hand, I felt relieved that it hadn't occurred to him before now to ask about my class background. On the other hand, I felt stung that he was calling attention to the difference between us, between me and most of the graduate students I knew. Because one thing was certain—if *he* had grown up working class, he wouldn't have asked me that question in front of other people, as if a lifetime of financial struggle were some kind of merit badge. Seth was someone I liked a great deal, but his comment made me see him differently. The burps and frayed clothing and Marxist ideology—suddenly I recognized all of that as rebellion, a form of atonement for the fact that his grandparents were loaded, that while he lived on the paltry salary of a graduate student, beneath him was a tightly-woven safety net.

After that incident, though, I began trying out the line, "I grew up working class." If you came from a working-class background, maybe it was logical that your vocabulary was less vast than it might otherwise have been. Maybe it made sense, too, that you hadn't studied as hard as you would have liked in college because of working full-time, that you hadn't started graduate school as soon as you wanted to because of still owing senior-year tuition, and that you hadn't known to study for the GREs. Maybe if you thought of yourself as coming from a working-class background, you might own up to that identity and claim the experiences it provided rather than distancing yourself from them. And maybe you could start to focus less on what you should have learned by a certain point in life and more on what you actually had.

The line "I grew up working class" gave me a certain cachet in graduate school discussions. I would throw it out there sometimes to distance myself from more privileged classmates or to bond with someone who, like me, was a first-generation college student. But it was one thing to identify my background and quite another to divulge the details of what that meant in my life.

One semester I took a literature seminar with eight other people, each one of us opinionated and stubborn. Personalities clashed all around the table, until our discussions began to sound like big family dinners where all the things people are really mad about get funneled into the way they ask for potatoes. This seemed especially true when we read Lorrie Moore's novel *Anagrams,* in which an embittered woman teaches writing at a community college. During the discussion, I said I thought the character was a parody of disgruntled academics, the kind who expect to teach at Harvard but find themselves instead at state universities or, God forbid, community colleges. I wasn't sure I believed my own interpretation of the book, but I had a bug on that week about disgruntled academics and elitism and some of the people around the seminar table, and I was using the novel to try to make a larger point.

Another student quickly responded. "It's not a question of whether she *views* herself as a failure," she snickered. "She teaches writing at a community college!" Everyone burst out laughing, the kind of long, hard laughter that separates us from them. I scribbled nonsense in my notebook so I wouldn't have to look anyone in the eye, having been put in my place in a way no one else realized. Perhaps I wasn't the only person in the room who'd grown up without financial security. But I was absolutely, without a doubt, the only person in the room who had gone to a community college.

And not just for a stray course or term. During my freshman and sophomore years, I'd studied full-time at the very community college where I later ended up working as a writing tutor. There, I'd taken Russian Literature with a man whose fur hat, high cheekbones, and animated eyes made him seem the embodiment of Raskalnikov. I'd read "Paradise Lost" with a woman whose breathless excitement made the poem feel like a mystery novel, and I'd studied Spanish with a man who was so absent-minded, disheveled, and morose that he might have stepped from the pages of a Lorrie Moore novel. Even so, he had inspired me to study abroad one summer and to think of myself from then on as someone capable of traveling the world.

What I hadn't gotten from those two years was the fluency I might have earned at a better school. I hadn't spent time with classmates whose vocabulary was broader than mine, who routinely used—because their parents did and their prep school teachers had—the kind of words I'd only seen on the page. I hadn't gotten as broad a liberal arts education as I might have elsewhere, and I hadn't been challenged, really challenged, in a way that would have made me rise to the occasion. But I had learned and been inspired, and my father had been able to write a check each semester for tuition, which meant a great deal to both of us.

Sitting in that graduate seminar, listening to everyone chuckle about the fate of community college teaching, I knew that with just a few words I could change the atmosphere in the room. I could say it kindly: "You know, my experience as a community college student was very different from what's described in this novel." Or I could be more abrasive: "Has anyone here—besides me, that is—ever actually gone to a community college?" I could point out the hypocrisy of an academic world where it's fashionable to study class difference but not to live it.

But of course I didn't. Between my vocabulary shortcomings and my verbal tic, I felt too vulnerable to own up fully to my story. During class discussions I often rehearsed what I was about to say—exactly as I had in Spain—before beginning to speak. But in the evening, at a party where I was relaxing with a glass of wine and letting down my guard, I might ask someone about their plans for "winter" break (in May) or about how soon they planned to take their "comprehensive insurance" (meaning comprehensive exams). I had learned to live with this quirk, for the most part, but I knew that if I outed myself in the seminar, I'd always fear that one of those students would approach at a party, hear me slip up, and raise an eyebrow. I hated that my language might betray me at any moment, might encourage people to judge harshly my background, my education, the place from which I'd come, and the person I really was.

In the end, though, if confidence means being comfortable with your failings, then a PhD program forced me to become confident in much the same way that living in Spain had.

Early on in Spain, my mind had been a sponge. During the first several weeks, I went from barely understanding anything people said to keeping up with conversations in ways that amazed me. But a few months later, my brain began to feel full. Vocabulary I'd gained in November failed me in March, and the closer I came to mastering the subjunctive mood of verbs, the more I hesitated when using the simple past tense. Lola noticed this and remarked that I didn't seem to be trying as hard anymore with the language. But I was trying. I made long lists of vocabulary words and went over them each night before bed. I stopped reading English books and started keeping a journal in Spanish. I hired a private tutor, who coached me in conversational skills, and except when I taught English classes, I lived entirely in

Spanish. Sometimes this seemed to be working, and I'd have long, philosophical discussions that felt like progress. More often, though, trying so hard made me weary, and when I was weary, words leaped from my mouth like psychotic fish diving into a grassy lawn.

And then a strange thing happened. A few months after I left Spain, I telephoned Lola when a letter to her came back as undeliverable. I felt nervous about calling because I assumed my ability to speak Spanish had deteriorated like an unused muscle, when in fact the opposite was true. After six months away from this language, speaking it was as effortless as drinking a glass of water. "I miss you!" we each shouted, our words tumbling over one another for twenty minutes. It felt as if a drainpipe in my mind had been clogged—by words and grammatical constructions and impressions and emotions. In the time since I'd left Spain, that mental pipe had finally cleared and I was more fluent than I'd ever been.

Something similar happened with English during my second phase of graduate school. I started the doctoral program obsessed with language, feeling a pinch whenever a student or professor used a word I didn't know, which happened daily, sometimes hourly. I tried to write down the unfamiliar words, but I no longer had the time or energy to look up each one, and my brain was so full I knew I wouldn't remember the definitions anyway. So I lived always with the fear of being caught out, of not being able to respond when I needed to because I didn't own the language in which I lived.

And then, eventually, it wasn't like this anymore. There were so many other things to worry about, like theoretical frameworks and choosing areas of specialization and, eventually, deciding to enter an MFA program in writing while finishing the PhD, that I got distracted from my lack of vocabulary. While I was distracted, many of the words I didn't know became familiar. I'd heard them used so often that they seeped into my own lexicon, becoming part of the way I expressed myself. I remember the very moment I understood this, the way sunlight fell in a thin rectangle across my kitchen floor, the way I leaned against the wall to catch my breath when I understood that my verbal self-consciousness had *abated* without my being aware.

Now I teach creative writing at an urban university where, nearly every term, a student confesses to me that his or her problem with writing has to do with vocabulary. It's been this way everywhere I've taught, at two state universities, at a small liberal arts college, and now here. "There are so many words I don't know," a young woman lamented recently, her cheeks flushing, "that I can't ever say things the way I want to."

I always assure these students that they have more than enough vocabulary right now to say what they mean, but that figuring out what they mean is very difficult. I tell them to pay attention to the words they don't know when they're reading or listening to someone speak. They don't need to look up every one, they don't need to memorize definitions. Instead, they should take notice, again and again, until a word feels less like an enemy than like a piece of fruit they want to pick up and bite into. I also tell my students the story of David Howard and the word *niggardly*, to help them understand that there's a power and a danger to words and that a large vocabulary is worth aspiring to as long as they remain suspicious of language in the process.

Every now and then in class, I'll say something, make a point in a way that seems perfectly obvious to me, and a hand will slowly go up. "What does *tenacity* mean?" the student will say, with a hint of apology in his tone, and my heart thrills each time. In my rush to explain, I often don't remember to say, "I'm glad you asked," but I am glad. And a little bit envious. I wish I had asked that question more often, had refused to skulk about with my head tucked into my shoulders, scribbling vocabulary words in a notebook.

These days I do ask. I live with a man who owns more words than I could ever hope to and whose manner isn't at all intimidating. Lying on the couch reading, I don't even consider getting up for the dictionary, I just hold my thumb against the page and call out, "What does *vertiginous* mean?" and he tells me, in the same tone of voice he'd use to tell me the time. I'm still learning words. Because I'm a writer, because I pay close attention to language on a daily basis, to its nuances and its trickery, I know I'll continue learning words for the rest of my life. I also suspect that until the bitter end I'll misuse even the words I know well because of some mysterious, uneasy relationship my subconscious mind has with language. But I'm less frustrated with that now, which I guess is a way of saying that, at least in English, I'm as fluent as I'll ever be.

Here's the proof: Recently I received an announcement for a conference panel called "Literary Entomologies." I cursed aloud when I opened the email because I thought I'd finally learned the difference between "the history of words" and "the study of insects." Then I read the description. Astonishingly, the panel was about the "intersections of insects and literary studies." I read that phrase twice, just to be sure, then let out a whoop and pumped my fist in the air.

Acknowledgments

For generous support during the writing of these essays, I am profoundly grateful to the American Association of University Women, the University of Iowa, the Rona Jaffe Foundation, the Millay Colony for the Arts, the Ragdale Foundation, the Illinois Arts Council, and DePaul University.

The following essays were published previously, sometimes in slightly different form: "The Queimada" (*Fourth Genre*, reprinted in *The Fourth Genre: Contemporary Writers of/on Creative Nonfiction*), "Grammar Lessons: The Subjunctive Mood" (*Crab Orchard Review*, reprinted in *Best American Essays 2006*), "Having Hunger" (*Organica Magazine*), and "In Praise of Envy" (*Georgia Review*). For information used in specific essays, I am indebted to *The Cave of Altamira* edited by Pedro A. Saura Ramos and *Guernica: The Biography of a Twentieth-Century Icon* by Gijs van Hensbergen.

The writer's life is not at all a solitary one, and I appreciate more than I can say the many friends and colleagues who have supported my work over the years. In particular, for their generosity and eleventh-hour insights, I wish to thank Yolanda Alonso, James Cañón, Susannah Mintz, Kieran Murphy, John Price, Becky Soglin, and Martha Wiseman as well as Holly Carver and everyone at the University of Iowa Press. I am enormously indebted to Carl Klaus for his years of generous, expert guidance and to Carol de Saint Victor for being the kind of writer and teacher I can only hope to emulate. Thank you to Francis Morano and Rita Morano, who very early on instilled in me the importance of learning. Above all, I'm eternally grateful to Kevin Quirk, whose patience and good nature are extraordinary.

sightline books
The Iowa Series in Literary Nonfiction